BECOMING A LEADER OF IMPACT

BECOMING A LEADER OF

HOW YOUR INFLUENCE CAN CHANGE THE WORLD **BRADEN DOUGLAS**

BECOMING A LEADER OF IMPACT
How Your Influence Can Change the World

ISBN   978-1-5445-1518-2 *Hardcover*
       978-1-5445-1517-5 *Paperback*
       978-1-5445-1516-8 *Ebook*

This book is dedicated to LeaderImpact.

Thank you for trusting me to write this. All proceeds from sales of this book will go directly to helping people around the world become leaders of impact through your work.

Stay the course. Run the race.

Impact is worth it.

CONTENTS

INTRODUCTION

WAKE UP

What am I doing here? It's 9:30 p.m. I stand up at my desk and look around. I'm the only one in the building. Everyone else at the posh Frito-Lay office on the seventh floor had gone home. I've been working fifteen hours straight, figuring out how to get people to eat more chips. I didn't have lunch. Again.

Why am I killing myself for this? Am I really going to spend my life being the chip guy? Seriously? To make matters worse, I loved it. The rush of it all: developing strategy, taking market share, making commercials, and working with smart people. But it's an empty life without a deeper purpose, and I knew it.

I drove the commute home along the freeway, sauntered up to my apartment, and sat on my bed. Across from me, on my black IKEA dresser was a mirror. I looked at myself with bags under my eyes and a wrinkled dress shirt. I didn't like what I saw and not just because I looked like crap at 11 p.m. I didn't like what I saw for my future. I loved marketing, but I wanted my life and career to matter and I couldn't see how I could reconcile the two. I felt this overwhelming urge to cry, so I just let it out.

I knew I needed to change. And I was determined to.

This was my wake-up call.

LEADING A LIFE OF IMPACT

Everyone, at some point in their life, will have a wake-up call moment. It's a moment when you have clarity on your purpose or realize your lack thereof. In pop culture, it's called a midlife crisis, but in reality, it will happen when someone is mature enough to reflect objectively. These moments can change a person's life and can lead to a fulfilling purpose, or they could lead to being divorced, buying a red convertible, and wearing unbuttoned dress shirts with gold chains across your chest.

In my case, I went on a personal journey after that night (as you'll read in chapter 8) and realized my purpose was helping leaders lead a life of impact. What does that mean? Over my career, being involved with LeaderImpact and in my marketing agency I get to work with a lot of leaders. These are entrepreneurs, owners, executives, rising stars, who are all striving to be successful. They might have wealth, but many of them are not happy. Not fulfilled. Their relationships with their spouses and kids are OK but not great. Some of them would call themselves Christians or have a faith, but it's not a vibrant faith, and it doesn't permeate into their lives let alone their business.

In some way or another, many of these leaders are facing their own wake-up calls. They want to have impact and more meaning and eventually to leave a legacy, but it's usually just good intentions with no plan. Even the term *impact* has become such a buzzword with varied definitions that it's become meaningless. It's nice to say, but how do you actually achieve it?

I wrote this book for them—for you. I'm not writing for everyone. I'm speaking to leaders—people who lead others, who aspire to and have been placed in positions of influence. Leadership is an active state more than it is a noun or position. Many of my stories and illustrations will be of business leaders who own companies or have top positions, but anyone can be a leader and have influence wherever they are in life and to whomever they can have influence. But this book is not written to convince someone to become a leader. There's enough of those books. I'm assuming that if you're picking up this book, you are already a leader in some form or another.

I'm convinced that leaders will impact the world more profoundly than any other group on the planet.

Leaders have the influence, skillset, affluence, and connections that are needed to move organizations, communities, countries, and the world toward a better, more positive outcome.

Think about that.

As a leader, you make strategic decisions every day to direct your resources toward an outcome. If you're a for-profit business, those outcomes are profit. If you're nonprofit, those outcomes are people or cause related. How well you do this and to the scale you're able to do it determines your impact in this world.

There has been no better example of the need for leaders of impact than through the COVID-19 pandemic.

In a matter of weeks, countries and people around the world were under pressure and lockdowns. The economy in many areas grinded down to a snail's pace. Thousands of people were sick. Millions of people were jobless. Millions more were scared, angry, and frustrated.

Health leaders worked tirelessly to care for the sick and protect their frontline workers. Governments scrambled to contain the virus and institute programs to help their citizens cope financially. Business and organizational leaders were trying to lead and communicate with their teams effectively, make difficult decisions, and strategize on new revenue streams or plan for what's next. Families were dealing with layoffs or, if they had jobs, were balancing the demands of work with the extra pressure of home, which for many also included homeschooling their children. The pressures and stresses were palpable.

All leaders were under a microscope. Everyone had opinions on how well or poorly they were leading. But there is no debate that leaders had impact. Their decisions could change the course of action for hundreds, thousands, or millions of people, and the impact of these decisions will stay with these people for the rest of their lives.

A leader of impact will make better decisions, handle pressure, and be more focused than a leader who's not. But you can't wait for a crisis to become a leader of impact. A crisis will only reveal what's already there.

Becoming a leader of impact is a life decision. It starts with intention and takes a lifetime to master, but you can get there.

Leaders are successful, but not all leaders have impact.

If you don't have a proper understanding of impact, you'll usually view success in terms of money or personal progression. When you make money, you will either keep it or pour it back into the business or organization to generate more with no real end point in sight. You will view progression and growth as a key driver for motivation, and you'll use your wealth to build an empire for yourself and a life of pleasure.

But what would happen if leaders all over the world started to think about success differently? Could we define success as the amount of impact we have and the amount of impact we leave?

Impact, as you'll learn, is about others. The definition that I'll introduce you to is that *impact* is influence that inspires others toward perpetual positive behavior.

If leaders became dialed in for the betterment of others, used their businesses and organizations for this purpose, and sacrificed for causes they felt drawn to, imagine the difference they would make. Imagine the legacies they would leave with their family, employees, community, and country.

This doesn't mean you'll live a life of poverty. But it does mean choosing a life of purpose over a life of pleasure.

This reality is not easy, but it's absolutely possible. There are leaders today living this way all over the world. You're probably even on the path to doing it yourself, but you just need a push. You just need the guidance, vision, and motivation to really live it out. And as you'll read, you can't do this alone. Just as the pandemic brought the world together, we're going to become leaders of impact together.

BOOK OUTLINE

This book is designed to change the way you think about your life and how you measure success. I'm going to challenge you on how you think about impact.

Here's what the book will cover:

- You're going to know what impact is and what it's not.
- The LeaderImpact Assessment will help you take stock of your life and what's happening in your core life areas. The assessment will benchmark you versus other leaders around the world to see where and how you stack up.
- You'll understand the LeaderImpact Model that integrates your professional, personal, and spiritual lives.
- You'll be inspired by stories of leaders who are making an impact and see that it's not complicated or boring or restricting.

We'll spend the first three chapters unpacking leadership, impact, and what a life of impact may demand of you in terms of struggle. Then we'll delve into the core of the book: the LeaderImpact Model. Chapters 4 to 10 will explore this model in depth, allowing you to grasp key ideas. In chapter 11, we'll bring it all together to discuss a holistic view of "leadership impact": we'll explore traits common to leaders of impact and show you how leaders have harnessed their talents and skills to truly change the world. Then, in chapter 12, we'll talk about what you probably know but haven't articulated: you can't do this alone. Our last chapter "Preparing for Impact" brings all these lessons together so that you feel energized and prepared to begin your journey.

I'm all in to help you.

My life's purpose is helping leaders find true success. I have been deeply involved in leadership development initiatives from as early as high school to university to my early career in marketing and now as an entrepreneur of one of the largest agencies in Canada and volunteering with LeaderImpact on a global scale.

I know what it's like to lead a demanding business and the stress and responsibility that come with it. I understand your limited effort and time. However, because I know your world, I'm also not letting you off the hook. Leaders make time for priorities that matter.

Writing this book was a priority for me. I made time in the early mornings and weekends because it's important. As a leader, you're going to decide what's important, and my hope is that your criteria for success starts to evolve to impact. You have the potential to change the world.

Be warned, though—this is not a regular leadership book.

The last thing I wanted to do was write another boring leadership book. There's enough of those, and I've read many of them, and I assume you have too. There are numerous leadership books and associations for leaders that address professional development and many on personal development. But addressing spiritual development and bringing all three together from the perspective of an entrepreneur is rare.

If you're looking for a leisurely read with the four points to success that tells you that you're awesome, put this down. It's not for you. Becoming a leader of impact is hard work. It's going to force you to think deeper and possibly change your thinking and life. This is for leaders who are driven—who want to succeed, are curious to learn more, and want to make an impact that leaves a legacy.

If that's you, it's time to wake up. Let's do this thing.

CHAPTER 1

IMPACT IS TRICKY

Have you ever had an idea that something was one way and later came to realize that you were totally off? When my wife and I moved into our first home, we didn't have neighbors yet. The house beside us was still in construction, and I waited expectantly for who those new neighbors would be. I always wanted to be that good neighbor. That neighbor who would cut the lawn for you, lend you a cup of sugar, shovel your walkway, and so on. Maybe the movie *The Truman Show* inspired me.

Finally, the day arrived when our neighbors moved in next door. A nice Filipino family with two young boys. A few days later, the dad was in the garden, and I thought this was my chance to introduce myself. I built up the courage, opened the door, and strolled over.

"Hi, congrats on moving to our neighborhood. My name is Braden," I said.

He was a small, stalky man that spoke gently, and you could tell he was shy but quite nice. "Hello," he said. "My name is Huijo, but it's tricky."

I couldn't really hear his response, but I swear he said his name was "Tricky." "Great! It's nice to meet you, Tricky. If you need anything, and I mean anything, just let me know," I said in a very enthusiastic reply.

I walked back inside and told my wife about my new favorite neighbor named Tricky.

For the next two years, I keep calling him Tricky because I actually thought his name was Tricky, and he never corrected me. I wasn't shy either.

"Good morning, Tricky!" "How's the fence coming along, Tricky?" "Hey Tricky, can I borrow your pruners?"

Finally, one day, his wife and my wife (Jen) both arrived home at the same time, and they struck up a conversation on the driveway. After some small talk, Tricky's wife mentioned to Jen, almost embarrassed, "Do you know that your husband calls my husband Tricky?"

"Yes," Jen replied.

"Well, his name is Huijo, and he doesn't like being called Tricky. Would you be able to mention that to your husband?" she said.

"Yes, for sure. I don't think he knew his real name," Jen commented, trying to save me a bit of dignity.

Jen came inside laughing as she put the groceries down on the kitchen island.

"What's so funny?" I asked.

"You know our neighbor Tricky. Well, his name isn't Tricky; it's Huijo."

"It's what?" I said, realizing that I've been wrong for this long.

"Huijo," she said.

"You mean I've been calling him Tricky for two years? And he hated it? And he didn't say anything?" I said.

I felt so stupid and embarrassed. Poor Huijo. All of this could have been avoided if I'd only known.

And here's the point for us.

Many leaders go through life thinking they are on the path to success only to realize late in life they were wrong. I hang out and work with leaders all the time, and many of them talk about leaving a legacy and wanting to make an impact.

But they don't know what impact means. They are doing activities, trying to be good people, but they don't really have an understanding of impact let alone a plan to achieve it.

Wanting to make an impact sounds good. Especially in today's world, it's very trendy to talk about having an impact and making the world better. But actually doing it is another level that most people never get to.

This is what we're going to work through in this chapter: understanding what impact is and what it's not so that you can understand it and start to focus on achieving it. This matters big-time, as we need people, especially leaders with influence, to be people who are impactful.

UNDERSTANDING IMPACT

Impact, as defined in the dictionary, is to have a strong effect on someone or something. Impact is not a specific action or an event alone. There are many people I meet who use "helping" interchangeably with "impact." *Helping* and *impact* are not the same.

For example, we all know the old saying, "Give a man a fish, feed him for a day. Teach a man to fish, feed him for a lifetime."

Giving the fish is *helping*. It's a charitable act made out of compassion or duty or guilt or some other motivation toward them. Teaching them to fish is *impact*. It changes their behavior and thinking in a way that can last their lifetime and even be passed on to others in the present and future generations.

Giving to a charity is helping. Inspiring people to care for that charity's cause is impact. Do you see the difference?

Impact is influence that inspires others toward perpetual positive behavior. Let me say that again: impact, as a leader should define it, is influence that inspires others toward perpetual positive behavior. As you can see, impact lasts.

John Maxwell, the famous leadership author of *The 21 Irrefutable Laws of Leadership*, says that "leadership is influence—nothing more, nothing less."[1] He's absolutely right, but it's not complete. Leaders influence *and* can create impact. Having influence doesn't automatically create an impact, but it does provide an opportunity for it. In essence, impact is influence that inspires.

For example, parents have influence, and their impact is seen in how their kids grow and behave. Managers and bosses have a great deal of influence and can impact their employees with what they teach, how they work and model behavior, and how they build into their people. The same goes for consultants, retail store employees, mayors, teachers, volunteers, instructors, coaches, captains of sports teams—anywhere you have a position of direct or indirect influence, there is an opportunity for impact.

To reinforce, impact changes or alters the way someone thinks and inspires them to lasting positive behavior. Leaders do influence, but not every leader produces impact.

I love sports, and many times, I was named the captain of my sports teams, such as soccer, volleyball, tennis, cross-country, among others. But I was a terrible captain. I felt the position or title of captain was earned for being one of the most skilled players on the team. I would yell at my teammates to "motivate" them to work harder. I would criticize their lack of work ethic or make comments on mistakes, thinking that this was going to motivate them and others to raise their game. I didn't know how a captain was supposed to act, and I genuinely thought I was a doing a good job as captain, especially if we won. It wasn't until I met Kevin Shonk that I realized I was dead wrong. The best part is that he probably doesn't even know how much of an impact he had on me.

I arrived at Olympic Volleyball camp in northern Ontario with one of my teammates, Stephan Larass. My position was setter, which meant I called the plays, touched the ball every second pass, and "set up" the hitters. Each camper was placed on a team with a player coach. The player coaches were older, experienced players, who would model and coach you as you played together as a team on the court. My coach was Kevin Shonk, a six-two power hitter with an amazing vertical jump who was an all-star for the Wilfrid Laurier University varsity team.

I walked onto the court, getting ready to call the plays, organize my team, garner their respect with my work ethic and ability, and lead them to victory. Then everything changed.

My player coach, Kevin, came bouncing on the court with an infectious energy. Smile brimming across his face, he approached each player with a low-to-the-ground sweeping high five and pulled the team together in the middle of the court.

"Are you ready for this?" he said.

"Yeah," we replied in a quiet and hesitant way, trying to understand what planet this Energizer Bunny was from.

"Come on. We're playing some ball. We're about to run wild on this other team. Shout it. Are you ready for this?" he yelled.

"Yes," we shouted back as we started bouncing a bit in unison with him in the court.

"I can't hear you," he continued.

"Yes!" we rocketed back in a loud thunderous voice.

"Still too quiet," he said.

"YES!" we yelled as hard as we could, as we're full-on jumping together in the court.

"Team 5 on three. One, two, three!" Kevin shouted.

"Team 5!" we all shouted back. We bounded back into our positions fired up, with big smiles, ready to take on the team across from us. That team could have been the US national squad, and we would have thought we could win.

That was good, but here's the best part. We started playing, and the game was close. A fast serve came over the net. A teammate in the back row passed the ball up to me in a good position. I set it perfectly to our outside hitter. He jumped too early and whiffed on the ball, and it landed into the net.

"Come on, Pat. You gotta focus!" I was about to shout. But before the words came out of my mouth, Kevin jumped in.

"Good try, Patty. You almost had it. Keep swinging. The next one is yours," he said, and gave him a high five and pat on the back.

Kevin looked over to me and gave me a wink. Kevin knew Patty should have crushed that set. What was he doing? Kevin knew that I should have been disappointed in Patty, but his response to Patty was not what I thought. Each play, regardless of the outcome, was met with positive affirmation.

The game continued, and we were deadlocked with this other team with only a few points to go. I was feeling the pressure. The ball came to me again, and I screwed up. I had set the ball to an empty space by the net, thinking a player should have been there. I gave the other team a crucial point.

"Sorry guys," I said with my head down.

"Don't even think about it. It happens. You're killing it out here. You've got this!" Kevin buoyantly shouted.

"Shake it off. You're carrying us, Braden," said Patty as he gave me a big high five.

We went on to win the next few points and ultimately the game. We were pumped. We all walked off the court celebrating. I eventually sat down and started taking off my court shoes. Kevin came over and plunked himself down beside me.

"Heck of a game you played out there, Braden," he said, still maintaining his big smile and energy.

"Thanks. It was fun. You rocked it too," I replied.

"What did you notice about the team or how I lead?" he asked.

"You helped the team focus and kept us on track. You made big plays when we needed it," I responded. I was a bit shocked at his question, as I didn't usually reflect too much on leadership after a game.

"The focus and outcomes are all secondary. I never think about those," he said.

"You don't?" I asked, not really believing him because every competitive athlete thinks about winning.

"Nope. My job as the leader is to get people to love the game, believe in themselves, and want to keep playing at the highest level on every play," he said. "The results will come. And even if they don't on that day, we'll want to keep training our tail off together, until they do."

That changed my entire way of thinking. I thought about what he said long after that day and still do.

Kevin made an *impact*.

If you ask my parents when I started to change and become a better leader, they will say sixteen years old at volleyball camp. I came home and became a new person.

Even today, as I lead a large agency of professional marketers, I try to inspire them to love marketing and to make a difference in the lives of others. This is how I combined a talent for marketing with having impact in the lives of others. (More on that journey will come.) I try to encourage my employees often so they believe in themselves. And I create a positive atmosphere that they are eager to show up to every day to do an amazing job for our clients and for themselves. The outcomes and performance will come when the confidence, belief, and desire is there.

I'm still not perfect (as my employees will attest to), but the impact of Kevin's intentional coaching changed the way I want to lead going forward in life. I'm reminded even now as I write this that we don't strive for perfection but, rather, for progress.

Everyone has the ability to impact.

I want you to say this to yourself, out loud, right now—yes, out loud—"Everyone has the ability to impact."

Do you believe that? This is the first step in becoming a leader of impact. You have to believe, in your soul, that you can have an impact on others. That you have the ability, and I would say responsibility, to be a leader of impact. If you don't believe this truth, you might as well stop reading now because I can't help you.

But if you believe this statement—and it's a simple statement—you'll have the ability to start something that will carry itself farther than you'll believe.

IMPACT CREATES MOVEMENTS

The measure of impact is in the size and scale of the movement that is generated. Impact can be created in intentional words or actions.

Consider Rosa Parks and her story of impact.

Rosa Parks was the secretary of the NAACP (National Association for the Advancement of Colored People) in the 1950s at a time when southern confederate states had adopted laws that segregated black and white citizens in public facilities, public transportation, and retail stores.

In 1955, around 6 p.m., after a full day of work, Rosa climbed onto the Montgomery city bus with driver James F. Blake—the same bus driver who forced her off the bus and into the rain a few weeks earlier because more white people boarded the bus, and there weren't enough seats for everyone. That was humiliating.

On this day, as more people loaded onto the bus, the white

section became full. Blake stood up from his driver's seat and walked down the aisle to the middle of the bus.

"Y'all better make it light on yourselves and let me have those seats," he told them as he looked down over the four black passengers. At first, no one moved.

"Let me have those seats," Blake said again, his tone becoming more stern. Three of the four passengers begrudgingly got up and moved to the back of the bus. But not Rosa. She stayed and moved closer to the window, digging in.

"If you don't stand up, I'm going to call the police and have you arrested," he warned.

"You may do that," Rosa responded.[2]

The police arrived and charged Rosa with violation of the Chapter 6 Section 11 segregation law of the Montgomery city code.

She wasn't the first person to boycott the city bus system, nor was she the key mastermind or leader of the equality movement, like Martin Luther King Jr., but her determination, will, and refusal to give in that day created an impact.

A few days later, after the thirty-minute trial that found Rosa guilty, the NAACP organized leaflets and distributed them to black churches and neighborhoods, asking for black citizens to boycott the buses on Monday, December 5. A front-page article in the *Montgomery Advertiser* helped spread the word.

The boycott strategy was a success in raising awareness and

uniting the black community to stand up for equal rights. This led to more boycotts and marches.

Rosa was a smart, caring, responsible woman, and the unfair treatment of her because of archaic laws sparked an injustice. Rosa impacted her community to take a stand. She didn't need compelling speeches or to be in a position of authority, but she dug in and became a force of influence. If Rosa could do it, so could we.

"People always say that I didn't give up my seat because I was tired, but that isn't true. I was not tired physically, or no more tired than I usually was at the end of a working day. I was not old, although some people have an image of me as being old then. I was forty-two. No, the only tired I was, was tired of giving in," said Rosa.

Rosa Parks became an icon for the civil rights movement. It would have a cost on her and her family, as she and her husband would lose good jobs because of the controversy, but there was no denying her impact.

The size of the impact is seen in the longevity of action that it continues to spurn. Movements are started from impact.

PERSONAL EXERCISE

Just plowing through a book is easy, but I want these ideas to stick for you. I've added some simple exercises to help you develop the thinking that will be needed to make progress. The first exercise involves writing down the names of people who have made an impact on you throughout your life. Making a list of some of the people who impacted you allows you to develop a keener sense of understanding of what impact looks like: the many shapes and forms in which impact occurs and how crucial or lasting that effect can be. It drives home the power of impact on a personal level.

As you reflect on your life, think about the people who have had a positive impact on you. Who were they? A teacher. Coach. Boss. Friend. Family. What did they do or say that has resonated with you?

Write the names of three to five people, and beside each name, write the impact they had on you. Try to be as concrete as possible. For example, if you had a teacher who impacted you, don't say, "They were great and made me feel good." That's vague and not helpful. Instead, try to remember the story or context that made you feel that way, such as, "My speech to the class was going terribly, and I started to cry, but my teacher stood up and congratulated me for having the courage to be vulnerable."

Do you have your list of people and the impact they've had?

Now, I want you to imagine the people in your life: family, friends, colleagues, neighbors, employees, teammates, suppliers, and anyone else.

How many of them, if they did this exercise, would put your name down? How many would have a story about how you impact them or have had an impact on them in the past?

We do this exercise with every LeaderImpact group I've led because it makes impact a reality that you can feel. And yes, this exercise is designed to make you feel guilty. I'm sorry. It's even hard for me, and I'm writing this book. But those feelings mean you don't like it, which is good. I hope it inspires you to take the challenge of becoming a person of impact more seriously, more intentionally.

KEYS TO REMEMBER

You have the ability to make an impact, but remember these three key points.

1. Impact is not the same as helping. It's about influence that inspires. That inspiration causes positive thinking, beliefs, and attitudes that lead to better outcomes for people.
2. Everyone has the ability to impact. It doesn't matter what role you have, who you are, or whether you are brilliantly skilled. If you have direct or indirect influence over someone, you can have an impact in their life.
3. Impact spreads and creates a movement. It's not a monumental action or occurrence; impact can happen every day if you are intentional and take hold of the opportunities with people. Small consistent steps with intention create momentum that turns into a movement.

Being in a leadership position and talking about impact is easy. Becoming a leader of impact is where it gets, well, tricky.

CHAPTER 2

LASTING IMPACT IS YOUR LEGACY ·

"Are we there yet?" I asked in a whining voice from the back seat.

"Almost. Fifteen minutes," my dad responded.

"You said that fifteen minutes ago," I said, clearly impatient.

Canada is a vast country. All you have to do is take a road trip, and you'll experience it. I was six years old, and we were traveling to Thunder Bay from Toronto. It took more than twenty hours of driving to get there.

"We're here," Dad said as he pulled off the highway to a lookout perched above Lake Superior.

My sister and I darted out of the car and ran toward the small crowd of tourists and onlookers. I ran up to the large monument and stared up.

"What happened to him?" I ask my parents.

"This is Terry Fox. He lost his leg to cancer and wanted to run across Canada to raise awareness and support for cancer research," my dad said. "He only made it to Thunder Bay before he died."

I remember seeing his statue. His prosthetic leg, which kind of freaked me out. But more vivid was his body posture and facial expression that was captured. It was pain mixed with determination.

"Why did he want to do that?" I asked.

"He hated what cancer took from him. He was young. He saw what cancer was doing to him and the other people suffering from it. He didn't want cancer to win—he wanted to fight back and provide hope," my dad explained.

"That's why he called his run the Marathon of Hope," my mom chimed in.

I've thought about Terry Fox often growing up, especially when our school would participate in the Terry Fox Annual Run in October. I'm a runner. Sometimes I would try to mimic Terry's one-legged run style to see what it would be like. I don't get far before I give up—it's hard.

If you only want to live a life of impact because of the rewards it may bring you, you won't make it far. It's hard work. Self-centered motivation doesn't last.

It's safe to say that Terry Fox's goal wasn't to have a monument created of himself in Thunder Bay, Ontario. It's a great statue of him, but it wasn't his point. Giving money alone is not impact. Acquiring fame or having people know who you are is not impact either. Neither is having your name on a university or hospital building considered a legacy. Statues, monuments, names, should only serve to remind people of the impact you want them to remember.

There are three important truths that you need to understand before you embark on or choose to live a life of impact.

IMPACT IS NOT ABOUT YOU

Do you care about something or someone more than the returns you could see? Would you pursue a life of impact even if no one remembered or knew what you did?

Imagine training your whole life in a sport, finally making it to the Olympics, and then sacrificing yourself so that your teammate can win. That's exactly what Colin Jenkins from Canada did. He came in dead last in the Olympic triathlon—on purpose. And no one knows who Colin Jenkins is.

Here's the background.

Simon Whitfield, a Canadian, had won gold at the 2000 Sydney Olympics for the triathlon and became a Canadian hero. Four years later in Athens, Greece, Whitfield came in a shocking eleventh place. Whitfield and the country felt a collective disappointment. Gearing up for the 2008 games in Beijing, at age thirty-three, the triathlon world was writing Whitfield off as too old to win or even finish in the top ten. Everyone knew this.

"I can't win on my own, but what if we did a team race?" Whitfield suggested.

Jenkins was a good triathlete but not considered a medal contender at all.

"Colin, we probably won't be able to medal on our own, but if we work together, we could accomplish something great for Canada. What do you say?" Whitfield asked.

"OK. I'm in," Colin responded.

Colin and Simon traveled to Beijing and were set for the start of the race.

The Olympic triathlon starts with a 1.5-kilometer swim, then a forty-kilometer bike ride, and finishes with a ten-kilometer run. Whitfield was an exceptional runner, but he needed help on the swim and bike ride.

The athletes lined up to start. *Bang!* The gun sounded to start the race. Jenkins sprinted ahead of Whitfield and ran into the water. He was close behind Jenkins, who plowed through the water and drafted Whitfield to make it easier for him to swim and conserve energy.

They emerged from the water and transitioned to the bikes. Jenkins, exhausted from the swim, ran to his bike and jumped on. Again, Whitfield was close behind him. Jenkins pushed through the wind at a great pace to draft Whitfield and make the ride easier. At the three-kilometer mark, Jenkins couldn't keep the lead pace any longer and dropped back. But that was all Whitfield needed him to do.

The athletes disembarked from the bikes and began the ten-kilometer run to the finish line. Whitfield was in fourteenth place as the pack began the run. His pace was exceptional. He began to gain ground with each kilometer and narrowed the gap. With three kilometers left, Whitfield was in a surprising fourth place but well back from the first three leaders. Then the energy he conserved in the swim and bike ride began to payoff. With one kilometer left, Whitfield mustered an incredible sprint pace. He passed the third-place runner. With the crowd behind him, he passed the second and then the first-place runner on the home stretch. Unable to keep a sprint pace the entire finish, the two runners behind him started to catch him, and it became a battle to finish.

The German powerhouse Jan Frodeno finally overpowered Whitfield with twenty meters to go to take gold, and Whitfield finished with an amazing silver medal.

Colin Jenkins, on the other hand, finished in fiftieth place. Dead last. As he ran the last leg toward the finish line, he looked up to see Simon Whitfield's name on the leaderboard as the silver medalist. He was ecstatic. He began high-fiving the spectators and cheering with the Canadian fans as he finished, knowing he helped accomplish something for someone else and for his country. And most people will never know or remember.

Some people criticized what Colin Jenkins did as not being in line with the Olympic spirit as an athlete. Others viewed him as having a good character or being a team player, and I think they would be right. It takes character to sacrifice the way he did so that his Canadian team could benefit. The impact Canadian sports and Simon Whitfield can have on people with winning an Olympic medal is far greater than coming fifteenth.

It takes strong personal qualities to live a life of impact. Everyone possesses those types of good qualities. Using and focusing them toward a greater good is impact. But not everyone makes that choice, especially when they may never see the benefits of their work.

That's why it's important to remember that true impact is not about you.

Is the cause or people you care about worth more than having the honor, rewards, or your name in lights?

IMPACT IS NOT ALWAYS EASY

Most leaders and brands want to be seen as someone or a company that makes an impact. When we talk about making an impact or are seen giving money, volunteering for a nonprofit, or taking place in a charitable race, people admire that. You'll have people complimenting you and being grateful for what you're doing. But why are you doing it? Are your actions motivated by the people you're helping, or are they focused on benefits you receive for participating? What if making an impact in public wasn't popular? What if it were the right thing to do but could bring you personal and professional harm? Would you still do it?

Two thousand years ago Jesus had a huge impact. Millions of people have put their faith in Him as God's son and built their lives on His teaching. But it sure wasn't popular. Jesus was constantly harassed and mocked by the leaders of his time. He was falsely accused of crimes he didn't commit so that he could be tortured and killed by an oppressive government. Do you think His mission mattered more than the consequence?

Was He thinking about the chapels or churches that would be built to honor Him in those moments? Of course not.

As the leader of a small group of followers, he had to model the life that is necessary to have a lasting impact. It's not easy. But it's worth it.

IMPACT HAS A COST

Hopefully by now, you're realizing that living a life of impact may not turn into the rewards, recognition, or fame some people think it will. On top of this, living a life of impact will cost you. I know. That's not very comforting. It will cost you your time. If you choose to focus on people with intention, you will need to spend time with them—time that could be spent in other areas or doing something else that you might enjoy more. It will most likely cost you money—investing in causes, trips, donations, gifts, and resources for others. This money could have been spent by you in other areas and on items or experiences that could have been really enjoyable too. Sometimes it costs relationships. Impact can sometimes mean standing up for ideals, morals, or ideas that not everyone agrees with. Sometimes those who don't see our point of view are the people closest to us, and those relationships can be damaged. Those types of costs hurt the most.

Isadore "Issy" Sharp is the founder of the successful Four Seasons luxury hotel chain. If you've ever stayed at a Four Seasons, you'll know just how good their guest experience and customer service is. They have service dialed in, and that service mindset was engrained into employees from Issy Sharp.

Issy and his wife, Rosalie, had four sons. Tragically, his youngest son Christopher died of skin cancer in 1978 at the age of eighteen. It was devastating for Issy and their family.

A short time later, Issy received a call from Peter Martin, his western regional vice president in Vancouver, Canada.

"Issy, there's a twenty-two-year-old young man named Terry Fox with one leg who is planning to run across Canada to raise money for cancer research. He's hoping to raise $1 million. Do you think the Four Seasons can help him out?" Peter asked.

"Sure. He and his team can stay at our hotels and eat for free along the route," Issy suggested.

"Great. He'll love that. Thanks, boss," he replied.

Issy was proud of Terry for taking this initiative, and he often thought of his son Chris when he thought about Terry's goal. A few weeks after the start of the Marathon of Hope, Issy and Rosalie gave Terry a call to see how it was going.

"Hi, Terry. We're proud of you. How's it going so far?" Issy asked.

Terry's voice was quiet with a saddened tone.

"It's OK, I guess. I just thought there would be a bit more publicity and awareness," Terry said.

Issy's heart was breaking. He knew how hard it was physically for an amputee to run almost a marathon a day. More than that, he knew how much Terry wanted to raise money and awareness to beat cancer. Terry's dejected mode was almost too much for Issy to handle.

"Let me see what I can do," Issy responded.

Issy hung up the phone and went into impact mode. He called Doug Hall, his director of advertising, to run a campaign called "Let's Make Terry's Run Count," and he challenged companies across the country to pledge two dollars for every mile he ran. If a thousand companies did this, they would be able to raise $10 million.

The ad campaign was just a modest success. As Terry was nearing Quebec, Issy knew he needed to do more.

He then sent one of his marketing people, Bev Norris, to Montreal to support the Cancer Society's efforts. Bev was able to have football star Don Sweet run with Terry into Montreal. When he entered Ontario, Bev and the Four Seasons let out thousands of balloons to welcome him with the governor general and a huge sign that read, "Welcome Terry. You can do it." They even had Terry do the ceremonial kick-off at a CFL game in Ottawa.

"One more thing," Issy quipped, "I'm going to organize a large luncheon in Toronto with successful business owners to hear Terry speak, raise money, and give him additional support."

"One hundred fifty people?" She asked.

"No, five hundred," Issy said with confidence.

And Issy and his team delivered. Almost all the invitees showed up to the luncheon.

Terry's quiet yet powerful speech at the Toronto Four Seasons

Hotel had the audience in tears. The business community was engaged and provided the support Terry Fox needed.

After 431 days, on September 10, 1980, as Terry was just outside Thunder Bay, Ontario, he was unable to keep running. Cancer had spread to his lungs, and there was no way he could keep pushing through the pain. They drove him to the hospital immediately. Up to that point, Terry had run 5,373 kilometers (3,339 miles). Less than a year later, Terry died. He didn't raise $1 million. His Marathon of Hope raised over $23 million that year and sparked a legacy.

Above Terry's hospital bed was a note pinned to the wall from Isadore Sharp:

> "You started it. We will not rest until your dream to find a cure for cancer is realized."

Issy and the Four Seasons' team, along with the Canadian Cancer Society, created the Terry Fox Run, an annual run to remember Terry Fox and to continue raising money for cancer research. It has been running every year since 1981, with millions of participants, and has raised over $300 million.

Isadore Sharp has been extremely successful. Four Seasons is an international icon for service and luxury, with over thirty thousand employees. However, in his book entitled *Four Seasons*, Issy's longtime friend said that the continued Terry Fox Run was the accomplishment Isadore was most proud of.

Would Terry Fox's Marathon of Hope have been as successful without the effort and investment from Isadore Sharp? Probably not. It cost Isadore and his company a lot of money, favors with business associates, and time. Impact has a cost. But it's worth it.

I was inspired as a young boy by seeing the Terry Fox monument and participating in the Terry Fox Run each year. Most people have no idea the role Isadore Sharp has played in Terry Fox's life, but it's exactly that type of leader who leaves a legacy.

Legacy is the length of time and the number of people affected by your impact. It's an intentional way to live out of a care for others. And it's hard work. Putting the needs, dreams, and hopes of others ahead of your own is not natural. That's why it inspires.

KEYS TO REMEMBER

If you want to be a leader of impact, remember these truths.

1. **Impact is not about you.** It's about putting others first and being intentional with them.
2. **Impact is not easy.** It's tough work to find the time, be intentional, or put your reputation on the line. If it's important, leaders find a way to push through, and that's what you need to do.
3. **Impact has a cost.** There is always sacrifice involved in being a leader of impact—donating your time and money that you feel you can't spare, connecting people, or sacrificing personal pleasure. The sacrifice is real, so don't be surprised when it starts to cost you something. Plan on it.

I'm just painting a rosy picture of leadership and impact, aren't I? I told you at the beginning that this is not going to be a book on how to be successful. This book is about being transformed to become a leader who impacts. It's a life decision. And it's about living an abundant life because that is what leaves a legacy.

Winston Churchill said it best:

> "We make a living by what we get. We make a life by what we give."

> **CHAPTER 3** ‹

BE YOURSELF. JUST BETTER.

It was hot. My legs were burning. My lungs were on fire. And I finally made it to halftime in the soccer game. We huddled up as a team. I was holding on to my water bottle tightly, spraying water in my mouth and on my face.

"Braden!" my coach called out.

The team turned and looked at me.

"What's going on? You're dogging it out there."

I looked at him, not really believing what I was hearing. *Really!* I thought to myself. I was busting my tail off and giving everything I had, and this out-of-shape coach was telling me I was dogging it. I was pissed off.

I fought back the impulse to argue and reason with him. He was the coach, and I loved playing and didn't want to be benched.

"You need to start playing hard. You're better than this. And I need more from you," he continued to yell. Three feet from my face.

I clenched my fists and bit my lip. The whistle blew to start the second half, and I played like a man on fire. I forgot about the pain in my legs or burning lungs. I was more aggressive, stronger on the ball, attacking, and relentless in my pursuit.

I didn't believe I had anything more to give. But I somehow gave my coach more.

Barry MacLean was my men's varsity soccer coach at Wilfrid Laurier University for the four years I was earning my degree. Remember Kevin Shonk from chapter 1? Barry's coaching style was nothing like that. He ripped into me on many occasions, pushing and challenging me to raise my game. And even though I hated it in the moment, it worked for me; Barry knew how to get the best out of me at that time in my life.

I felt like the drummer in the movie *Whiplash* who gets emotionally abused and pushed but finally raises his game. Just not as dramatic. I was a walk-on for the varsity team. Unlike the majority of the players on the team, I wasn't recruited to play. I just showed up to the open tryouts at the beginning of my first year of school.

"You're not the most skilled, Braden, but you're fast. I want you on the team, but you probably won't play," Barry said in my first year.

He was right. I never played in a single game that first year. I wasn't even on the bench. It was worse than that. I never actually suited up in uniform. This is what sports teams call "redshirting." I was on the roster but only practiced with the team, and many times, I didn't travel with them on longer away games. It was humbling.

You practice, work hard every day while balancing a full school course load, and never get to play. There were a couple of other guys in this position too. Some stuck it out. Others quit. What would you do?

I stuck it out, but I knew I needed to be better. The coach kept me for my speed, so I was determined not to lose a single running drill. When the coach made us run suicides, which is sprinting back and forth between lines on the field, I rarely—if ever—lost. Guys would take turns resting between sets to save energy to beat me. I took it as a challenge and beat them each time.

My team became the practice squad. The benchwarmers and redshirts. We would go up against the starting players in scrimmages and drills. We wanted nothing more than to crush them. Other teams might take it easier on their own players or not try as hard in practice as they would in a game. Not us. We were relentless and, many times, more aggressive with our own team than when we played the opposition. There was a shoving match, a bloody nose from an elbow, or a fight at practice every few weeks. It was intense, but once practice was over, we were friends.

This relentless and competitive culture paid off, and the team become sharper and better prepared. I improved faster as a player and eventually moved up the depth chart to start games in my third year. I was then named captain of the team in my fourth and final year. To top it off, we won two national championships in those final two years I played. The only time in the university's history that they have won the men's varsity soccer championships.

Barry demanded more. I gave him more and became a better player and person because of it. He didn't treat every player in this manner. As a seasoned coach, he knew how to motivate certain players. He would be soft and empathetic to some and to others, like me, he was in your face. He cared for his players, but his job was not to win friends; he was there to prepare his players to win.

And to win and be a champion requires more.

That's what the world wants from you too: more. Because that's what impact takes and because you're capable of it. Your family, friends, colleagues, and employees would all gladly have more from you too. Yes, that sounds daunting and exhausting, but you can do it.

BE YOURSELF. JUST BETTER.

The common teaching and mantra is to be yourself. It's true that we want to be authentic and not pretend to be something or someone we're not. That's obvious. I think everyone's unique abilities and perspectives are what make this world richer. The point I want you take away is to never settle. There are no limits to how people can learn and develop. I want to say that again: there are no limits to how people can learn and develop. That's where you get better. Don't be afraid of being pushed.

Jesus was about thirty years old when he started to walk from village to village teaching people about God and how to live. He gathered a small group of people to train them to do what he was doing, which were his disciples. They were a mixed bag of fishermen, a tax collector, rebel, thief, and other simple guys that you would not expect to be with a great teacher.

As Jesus was teaching a crowd of people in a village, he told them this story and asked the people to think about its meaning.

> One day a farmer planted seed. As he scattered the seed, some of it fell on the road, and birds ate it. Some fell in the gravel; it sprouted quickly but didn't put down roots, so when the sun came up it withered just as quickly. Some fell in the weeds; as it came up, it was strangled by the weeds. Some fell on good earth and produced a harvest beyond his wildest dreams.[3]

What do you think this story is about, and how does it relate to becoming a person of impact?

It's an interesting parable, and if you're struggling with it, don't feel bad. Jesus's disciples had no idea either and had to ask Him about its meaning later that night privately.

You are the soil, and the type of soil you have cultivated in your life will determine what you do with new ideas and messages (which are the "seeds") and if they will produce anything meaningful. There are four types of soil/people: road, gravel, weed-filled, and good earth.

- **The road is hard ground.** You're fixed on your position and way of thinking about a subject, and you're not open to new ideas or suggestions. The seed is not getting through, you dismiss it outright, and it's forgotten. Gone.

- **The gravel is mixed soil.** You read the latest article, try the new fad diet hoping for better results, come back energized from a conference, but the change or new perspective doesn't last. The diet is gone once someone pokes a hole in it. The advice you were so keen on is abandoned when a close friend or family member laughs at it. It doesn't become rooted in your life, and so it fades away.
- **Weed-filled soil is good soil, but it's full of distraction (weeds).** There are too many competing priorities, too many avenues you want to explore; or the hard work of being disciplined, delaying gratification, or swimming against the current of popular culture is too much. The new idea or message is drowned out and ineffective. You have good intentions but nothing to show for it.
- **The good earth in the parable is the best soil.** It receives the message openly, internalizes it to grow strong roots, removes distraction, commits to it, and eventually sees the results that are far greater than could have been imagined.

Jesus was speaking about his message on knowing God. But the parable applies to all messages. There will be some people who never choose to embrace a life of impact. Others might just reject the idea outright as too simple or not for them. Some may get a new perspective but quickly forget about it as the busyness of life takes over. But there will be a few who get it. These are the leaders who are ready for change, ready to take on the challenge, ready to get together with others who think the same and live a life of impact. They are the ones who will look back and see the amazing results of their hard work.

The question we all have to ask ourselves regularly is: What type of soil are we going to be? Can we be ourselves, just better?

STRUGGLE IS PART OF THE PROCESS

Living a life of impact requires you to be better. It's hard work, and it doesn't happen quickly, which is why I believe more people aren't doing it. It's much easier to live life for yourself and focus on what you need to do to survive and live for personal pleasure or lifestyle. No one wants to struggle.

My dad spent forty years as a landscape architect for two city municipalities. In the early 1990s, he designed the landscape for a local school and decided to put in a butterfly garden with a specific assortment of wildflowers that would attract butterflies. He created educational signage on the life stages of a butterfly, and the school could create curriculum for the students to learn about these beautiful insects. The idea took off, and more schools wanted my dad to create these butterfly gardens for their schools. He became the butterfly guy.

After a hockey game one day, my dad and I were driving past a school that had one of his butterfly gardens on it.

"Hey, Braden, want to check out a garden I put in at this school?" he asked.

"No, not really," I replied. There's not a lot of teenage boys that jump at these opportunities, and I was one of them.

"Great!" he said, as he turned a sharp left into the school parking lot.

We got out the car and walked to the side of the school where the garden was located. It was full of wildflowers growing in big boxes with pathways throughout. I had to admit that I was impressed. I walked to a part of the garden where I spotted a cocoon hanging from a tall plant. I leaned in close and could see the caterpillar wiggling around. It looked ready to break free and was trying to get out. I started to slowly pull at the cocoon.

"Don't touch that!" my dad yelled out.

"Why not? It wants to come out," I responded.

"The caterpillar needs to struggle out of the cocoon in order to build the right muscles that enable it to fly," he said. "If you help it, it'll end up falling out of the cocoon and become lunch for a predator."

"I see," I said.

I thought I was doing something helpful. I didn't realize that struggle was necessary for the butterfly. It's one of these lessons that I never forgot from my dad, and I'm truly grateful that he took the time to turn left that day into the school parking lot.

Struggle is part of the process of becoming better. It's uncomfortable and hard work, which is why most people plateau and don't improve. I'm sure the caterpillar would have welcomed the help. That's only because it can't see the bigger picture or have the wisdom to know what's best.

How often are we like a caterpillar? Life gets hard. Your business or job is going through a tough season. Money is far too tight. Relationships with your spouse or kids or extended family are difficult. These are real struggles. It's easy to complain or get trapped in self-pity or blame others and sometimes even blame God for the situation we're facing.

It's actually in these moments when we experience the greatest growth as a leader. We're developing mental muscles on how to persevere, learn, and grow so that we can impact others who will face similar situations in their own careers and lives.

We've probably all heard the quote "No pain, no gain." I know it's true, but in my tough moments, I change this statement to be: "Focus on the gain to get through the pain."

If you continue to focus on the outcome you're going to see at the end, the pain in the process becomes much more manageable. Picturing your new weight loss and higher energy gets you through the current diet. Seeing a great and vibrant marriage for yourself can get you through the dry or rough patch that you might be currently facing. Envisioning the business thriving, profitable, and helping people gets you through the late nights and current setbacks that you face.

In many cases, we can't always change our circumstances, but we can change our perspective and our attitude toward them. We can realize that struggle is an important part of the journey—a necessary one. And we can embrace it.

DON'T BE A LEADER WHO RESCUES

Just as struggling is important for your self-growth, it's important to give others the space to fight their own battles. This can be tough for most of us. If you see someone drowning, yes, you should rescue them. But what if they keep drowning every week, and they look to you (or others) to rescue them each time? It's not that bad, is it? You care about them. You're capable of doing it. They're safe because of your actions. So what's the harm?

In psychology, a dependent relationship or dependency occurs when you do something for someone that they are capable of doing themselves. You will not become a leader who impacts at a high level if you create dependent relationships and are not able to delegate. It limits your ability to multiply and get scale.

As a leader, helping can hurt, and it's been one of the lessons that I've struggled to learn. Just as I wanted to help the caterpillar out of the cocoon when I was a teenager, I realize that, from time to time, I help my employees and even my kids when I shouldn't. When I'm feeling under stress or pressure, I become a leader who rescues, and I hate it.

For example, in my company, we hire a lot of smart, promising employees. Some of them are young with limited experience, and others have more years under their belt, but most are pretty green when it comes to working at an agency. It's a fast-paced environment and requires you to produce quickly and with high quality. If I give a new employee a marketing strategy to complete, I usually get the first draft back, and it stinks. I give some feedback and try to coach them in the right direction. The deadline is coming up for the client. I meet with the new employee again to review their second draft. It's better but still not great. Now the employee and I are both feeling the pressure because we care about doing a good job.

"Let me take it from here," I say to them.

"Great. Thank you," they say in desperate relief.

I work late into the evening and get it done. It's a great strategy, and we present it to the client, who loves the ideas and direction.

The next strategy project comes up. This employee creates a first draft, and it's similar to the last first draft of the strategy from before. It needs a lot of work. In the essence of time and wanting to do a great job, I take it over again. And the cycle continues.

You might be thinking that this cycle and my behavior is crazy. It is crazy. It's insane actually. Thinking I'll get better results by doing the same thing. Yet many leaders I work with enable employees or people to stay in dependency on them. It might feel good to be needed and to know that you're doing a great job, but it limits. It impedes growth of the organization and for the individuals involved. Yes, it even stifles the growth of the leader as they are stuck doing activities that others are capable of doing themselves, and they can't work or develop other areas.

My first marketing position was with Procter & Gamble while I attended university over two summers. I remember feeling proud that I landed a coveted position with a prominent company at such a young age. I was placed on the Bounce and Downy fabric enhancer brands in the laundry division. My manager was a talented, smart, and approachable guy named Jeff Straker. He was also openly gay, which wasn't as common in the late 1990s, so he had a strong and confident demeanor about him.

"Here are the assignments I need you to complete," Jeff said to me in his office.

"Great. These will be good assignments and will keep me busy this summer," I said with confidence.

"Summer? For this week," he replied in all seriousness.

"Oh, right. Absolutely." My eyes must have been bulging out of my face like a deer in headlights.

"Braden, make the progress you can and check in with me each day for five minutes to ensure you're on the right track. Get at it," he said.

I left his office and started working on the first assignment. Determined to make great progress and show my new manager that I was a star, I worked late into the night. I came back the next morning to check in and hear the praise of my progress.

He ripped it apart.

"Your rationale is not sourced. The language is passive. The structure is erratic. It's too verbose," he said as he took his red Bic pen out and marked up the whole report.

My heart was beating fast. I was frustrated, confused, and needed help. But the help never came. I worked on it again until late in the night and checked in with Jeff the next day.

"It's better but still needs a lot of work," he said.

I was dying right then. I was the valedictorian of my high

school. I had good marks in university, but I was not ready for this "real world." I was trapped in the P&G cocoon. I was struggling to find a way through this. Jeff never helped me through that cocoon. At the time, I hated it. I blamed him for not helping me more and taking some of the burden off me.

But I made it through. I eventually improved and became much more efficient. I returned to school that fall and was markedly better prepared than other students. My work ethic was stronger, enabling better performance and setting a foundation for a successful marketing career.

Jeff didn't rescue me. And the struggle made me better.

As you read this book and think about your life as you process the next sections, I want you to know that I'm not going to rescue you. The world needs leaders, like you, who will have an impact on others. You will never get there if you don't do the hard work or struggle through the tough questions.

This is not a how-to manual in which I give you the five steps to make an impact. That's not how real life works. It's not how leaders are made either. The purpose is to provide insight, inspiration, and keys to help you determine how you're going to do it. You will have a unique impact in the world, and my job is to try and squeeze it out of you.

KEYS TO REMEMBER

I want you to be yourself, only better. So remember:

- You have to be committed to the process and doing the hard work.

- Embrace the struggle in the cocoon. It's necessary for the transformation.
- Don't look to be rescued or to take the shortcut. And don't rescue those who are under your own leadership.
- Envision the gain to get through the pain. Keep the end in mind. Becoming a leader of impact matters to those you care about, and it will matter to the world.

The higher you climb as a leader, the bigger the struggles tend to be. This idea was captured beautifully by James Allen in his book *As a Man Thinketh*: "He who would accomplish little need sacrifice little; he who would achieve much must sacrifice much. He who would attain highly must sacrifice greatly."

Accept the struggle. Lean into sacrifice. Learn from both. It's developing your muscles so you can fly even higher.

CHAPTER 4

THE LEADERIMPACT MODEL

I was standing up front at a hotel ballroom in Calgary, Alberta, answering questions from a few people after a keynote I gave to leaders in the area.

"I get leadership, but what does impact really mean for me?" a young leader asked me.

He was tall and well dressed with a dark complexion that highlighted his Middle Eastern origin. I could tell by how articulate and confident he was that he came from a good home and was determined to be successful with his life.

I don't remember the full answer I gave him, but I know it wasn't good. It was full of jargon, like "empowering," "grit," "influence," or a myriad of other trendy leadership buzzwords. Sometimes if we say enough of those words with enthusiasm and conviction, it usually satisfies people, and we can get away with it.

"OK," he said politely. "Thanks for your time." And he walked away, but I knew he wasn't satisfied.

I couldn't walk away from this.

I knew this young leader, like many leaders, genuinely wanted clarity to the question of impact. It was a question that I kept chewing on in my mind, especially knowing that I had another speaking engagement coming up in a few weeks to another group of leaders.

Finally, one early morning, I was in my home office planning out my upcoming talk. I start my planning by thinking about the audience and organization that's invited me to speak. In this case, the organization was LeaderImpact. An organization that had been gathering, challenging, and supporting leaders in groups and events to think about their lives holistically in order to make an impact that changes the world. I've been volunteering with them for over a decade, and they're whom I'm partnering with on this book.

What did LeaderImpact want to accomplish with this event I was speaking at? Who is the audience? Where are they in their lives? What's going to help them succeed?

I couldn't shake the question from the young leader in Alberta. I wrote down one statement: "Where does impact come from?" I wrote down "outcome" but quickly crossed it out. The outcome is not the goal. "Who is a leader who has impact on others?" I then thought about great leaders in history and other leaders who have had an influence in my life. I wrote down three points and drew a circle around these points and realized I was creating a Venn diagram.

Over the next few weeks, I started collecting feedback on this theory from various people. I further refined it. With the diagram complete, I used it as the main content in a keynote presentation at the event. Just so you know, this is a dangerous thing to do, as new material is always harder to present as a keynote. The result? Surprisingly amazing. It was clear in my mind as I presented it, and the feedback from the LeaderImpact staff and the leaders in attendance was strong.

We were onto something. Over the next year, I, along with LeaderImpact staff, several high-level leaders, and executive coaches further refined it. The model is now incorporated as a core "Foundations" training for leaders when they join LeaderImpact.

It's simple but not easy. Meaning it's simple to understand and grasp the concept but not easy to implement into your life. I guess you can say it's easier said than done, which is why it's highly recommended you be in community with others as you work through it.

THE LEADERIMPACT MODEL

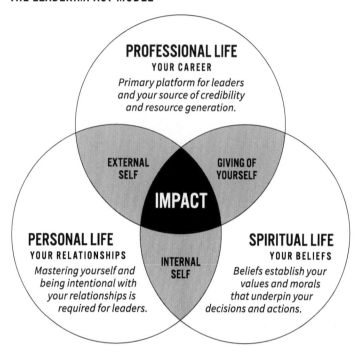

EXTERNAL SELF
YOUR IMAGE

How you want the world to see, understand, and engage with you.

INTERNAL SELF
YOUR CHARACTER

Your thoughts and motives in your behavior towards others.

GIVING OF YOURSELF
YOUR CONTRIBUTION

Aligning your career with your beliefs provides deep intrinsic motivation and longevity.

IMPACT
YOUR LEGACY

The integration and optimization of your Professional, Personal, and Spiritual Lives.

The LeaderImpact Model is based on the premise that IMPACT occurs when a leader's personal, professional, and spiritual life are fully integrated and optimized.

It's not about *what* you do but rather *who* you are that matters. Let me say that again because leaders typically place a massive emphasis on what they do. Impact has more to do with *who you are* than *what you do*. If you're a leader who makes an impact, you'll do that regardless of your role, activity, or job.

My hope is that this book helps you shift away from *what* to *who*. Impact is not performing a list of activities in a formula to produce a certain type of result. It's a who question first. Who are you? Do you desire to be a leader who has impact? How are you becoming a better person? A better leader? Then it's "Who are you having an impact with? Why are they important to you? Why is having an impact with them important for the world?"

The LeaderImpact Model and subsequent examples and stories are only there to help you work through this so that the thinking and philosophy takes root in your life. Once the root is strong, then growth can happen, and that's when you see results.

Let me walk you through the model at a high level before we go into each area in detail in chapters 5 to 10. There's a lot here, so take your time going through the sections. Make sure you have a grasp on what is being said. The following chapters will explore maximizing each area to create impact, but this high-level summary is the conceptual heart of the model.

PROFESSIONAL LIFE

This is your career. On average, you will spend ninety thousand hours or roughly one-third of your life at work. If you're like me, you might even spend more than that. And this is not even counting the time you're thinking about work when you're not there. With that much time invested into your career, you can see why and how your identity can become what you do. It's also a critical area for leaders as your platform for credibility and influence over others typically emerges out of your profession. Abraham Lincoln wasn't an admired leader because of his moral stance on issues like slavery or because he was a good husband. It was because he was the president of the United States and had a major influence in millions of people's lives. His strong moral ethics and personal characteristics propelled his impact further, which changed the Western world.

Regardless of where you are in your life and career, you can be focused on making an impact. The better professional you are and the higher the position you attain, the bigger the platform or opportunity for impact. Therefore, it's critical to always be learning and honing your skills and knowledge so that you can have a bigger impact in the world.

PERSONAL LIFE

This is characterized by your relationships. It starts with knowing yourself and how you behave, think, and take care of your well-being. It then moves to the relationships you have with others—from colleagues to friends to family and beyond. Mastering yourself and being intentional with the relationships in your life is the starting point for impact. If you can't have an impact on those closest to you, you won't have impact on the masses. It starts small and cascades out.

SPIRITUAL LIFE

This is your beliefs. The values and morals that underpin

your decision-making have a tremendous influence on your professional and personal life outcomes. This area drives and determines your motives and definitions for success and for impact. Every leader chooses a belief system to follow, whether they consciously know it or not. This was a journey for me, like it is for many others. When I understood who God is and why a real relationship with Him matters, I was finally able to see past myself to the needs of others. Impact is not about you. You can know that at a head knowledge level, but that idea has to be felt in the depth of your soul in order to be lived out every day.

The intersection between these life sets and how they relate to each other will provide deeper insights to help you as a leader.

EXTERNAL SELF (PROFESSIONAL AND PERSONAL)

This is your image. It's created from your Professional and Personal Life and determines how people see, understand, and engage with you. It's a collection of interactions and information that forms an opinion of your reputation or identity. For example, Mother Teresa creates a very different image in your mind than, say, Donald Trump, even though you most likely have never met either of them. The External Self is connected to *what* we do in our lives. All of us try to manage our ideal image for the outside world. Social media and technology is the new outlet to allow this to happen, and it's pretty amazing to see. But there is a downside. What image are you trying to create? For whom? How are you comparing yourself to others? Are you good enough?

If you are building an image for personal gain and accolades, it will leave you anxious, depressed, and desperate. No one wants to see people striving for likes on social media or following leaders who are politicking inside organizations to get ahead. Managing and building an authentic identity on a foundation of purpose is critical to impact.

INTERNAL SELF (PERSONAL AND SPIRITUAL)

When your Personal and Spiritual Life come together, it forms your Internal Self. This is your character. If the External Self is about *what* you do, your Internal Self determines *why* you do it. Your desires, motives, thoughts, and ambitions are all directed by your values, beliefs, and spiritual worldview. Who are you when no one is around? What do you think about? Why do you really want to have more?

If your motives to make an impact are not coming from a deep place of care for others and a sense of purpose, you will never have lasting impact.

GIVING OF YOURSELF (PROFESSIONAL AND SPIRITUAL)

When your Spiritual Life engages your skills, knowledge, and experience from your Professional Life, this is when people benefit from the gift of your leadership. This is your contribution to the world. Giving of Yourself forms *how* you are doing things and living out a life of impact. This doesn't mean you need to be working in a nonprofit organization or can't be focused on profit or results as a business. Every cause must have resources to succeed. Throughout history, leaders have provided connections and large sums of money to propel great causes forward. It's an amazing privilege but requires great sacrifice to give of yourself in great quantity.

When you understand and accept your purpose, your motivation and drive is balanced with a compassionate mindset, a care for people and the environment, and a desire to use profit and influence for impact.

IMPACT (THE FULL COMBINATION)

This is the fully engaged intersection of your Professional, Personal, and Spiritual Life. It's an integrated life. This is *what* you do, *why* you do it, and *how* you're doing it, which creates *impact* in the lives of others. Your influence causes positive thinking, beliefs, attitudes, and actions that lead to better outcomes for yourself, your family, friends, colleagues, community, and society at large. Wouldn't that be amazing? Wouldn't this be worth living for? Sacrificing for?

Impact is ultimately the legacy you leave to this world.

Please remember that the LeaderImpact Model is merely a framework to help you, as a leader, think about the components of your life in order to influence positive thinking, behavior, and decisions. There are countless books and authors who have helpful frameworks. In my experience, it's not what model you choose to follow that matters. It's actually doing the work within these frameworks that creates results. Action and execution is paramount. The framework just helps communicate and organize the information so that it can scale to hundreds of groups and thousands of leaders who want to become leaders of impact.

The next chapters will start your journey assessing and understanding that impact is the result of an integrated life. As I've said before, understanding IMPACT is simple, but living it out is not easy. My role is to help you develop and grow so that you can be the kind of leader who has impact.

THE LEADERIMPACT ASSESSMENT

You've heard the Chinese proverb, "The journey of a thousand miles starts with a single step"? It's a reminder that even though the journey is long, you just have to start, and the immediate actions are small. This is your life. It can be for a short or long time, but you have to take action. Starting with small steps is the best way. The fact that you're still with me up to this point means that you're ready to take the steps necessary to make a difference. The biggest decision to make now is in what direction you go and what areas you focus on.

The LeaderImpact Assessment can help you with this. At the back of the book or online at LeaderImpact.com is an assessment that was developed to help leaders assess their lives in context of the LeaderImpact Model. The questions are designed to help you think about your three life areas (professional, personal, and spiritual) in a deeper way and to provide a practical benchmark to track progress. You can answer these questions in the book or online. The online version gives you an output immediately and compares your score with leaders from around the world so you can see how you stack up. (Oh, come on—I know you have a competitive side, and you're interested in seeing your stats.) Complete this survey before you move on to the next chapter; it will give you a keen understanding of what kind of leader you are now and help you relate to the concepts explored in the rest of the book.

Once you've completed the survey and are ready to dive into the model, keep reading.

CHAPTER 5

PROFESSIONAL LIFE

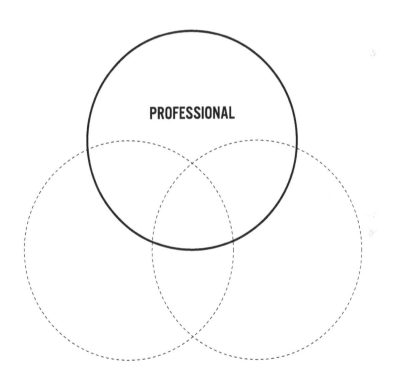

PROFESSIONAL

I was on the track-and-field team in high school. I was a runner and focused on the 800- and 1,500-meter distances. If you've ever trained for running, it's not the most fun event to train for. You basically just run—a lot. One day after school as I was running around the track, I kept noticing all the field event athletes having a great time.

"Here are these guys having a blast throwing around heavy objects and jumping on mats. That seems like a far better idea than running around and around for an hour," I said to myself.

Off in the corner of the field, I noticed the pole vaulters. They were reaching big heights and cheering loudly when one of them cleared the bar. They weren't huge physically, they had a spot on their team for another member, and I thought that might be a great event for me to try.

After practice, I mustered up the courage and approached my track coach to see if I could join the pole vault team.

"Coach Watkins, do you think I would be able to try pole vault?" I asked.

Coach Watkins was a strong, stern, female track coach who looked like an embattled rugby player and had a personality that was a bit cold.

"I don't think so. It's not an event for you."

"Please. I really want to do it," I begged.

"OK. Fine. As long as it doesn't conflict with your running events, and you complete your running training before you practice the field event," she responded. I could tell she didn't like this idea, but I was elated.

"No problem," I said confidently. I ran over to join the vaulters and tell them the great news.

It turns out pole vaulting is hard. Definitely harder than it looks. You have to sprint about thirty meters toward the jump area while holding a twelve-foot pole and then plant it perfectly, using your momentum to send you straight up into the air about three to five meters. While in flight, you need to angle and change your body to reach over the bar and land on your back in the mats.

It looked easy, but I couldn't seem to get it. That's a nice way of saying that I was never able to make it over the bar, even at the lowest height. Despite my lack of natural talent, the pole vault team was great. They were patient and coached me through it. I still couldn't clear the bar, but I was so close.

The regional track-and-field meet was fast approaching. Coach Watkins came up to me after practice one night.

"We can register three pole vaulters for your age category. Have you been able to clear the bar?" she asked.

"Yep. You bet," I lied. Even as the words were coming out of my mouth, I knew I shouldn't have said them.

"Great," she said. "You're in."

It's like they always say in business, "Fake it till you make it." I couldn't make the height, but I was determined to. For the next week, I practiced hard. But no matter how hard I tried, I wasn't able to clear the bar, and I didn't want to admit failure to Coach Watkins.

The day of the track meet, I looked the part. I had my school signet on and my super short running shorts that I used for the running events. They made me look like a professional pole vaulter, and I needed all the self-confidence I could get.

The event started, and there was a good crowd gathered around, as the pole vault is pretty fun to watch. Each vaulter was called by the event judge and then jumped over the initial height with ease and grace. I knew I could do it.

"Braden Douglas. E. L. Crossley. First attempt," the judge called out.

I was ready and focused on the lane ahead. My pole angled up in the perfect position. I sprinted down the lane with determination, planted the pole, and jumped straight into the bar, which fell down, making a gonging sound off the concrete. I was embarrassed. I looked down at the bottom of my foot as if something magical had tripped me and caused me to miss the jump.

I walked back to the start of the lane, passing Coach Watkins along the way.

"What happened?" she asked in disbelief.

"Just tripped on something," I said. And lied again. I really wanted that to be the truth.

I was the only jumper who missed the initial height. Now every athlete and onlooker was staring at me to complete the jump and move on to the next height.

"Braden Douglas. E. L. Crossley. Second attempt," the event judge called out again.

I took a deep, exaggerated breath in and let it out slowly. I saw the bar ahead and ran down the lane toward it. My track team was cheering me on. I planted the pole in the exact spot. The pole bent and sent me straight up into the air. I was flying. But not forward. I landed awkwardly straight down onto the lane and fell backward. The bar still in its position and everyone staring at me in disbelief and the odd chuckle from the opposing athletes.

I sauntered back to the start of the lane. Again. Coach Watkins had her hand over her mouth and was looking straight at me. She didn't need to say anything, as the look in her eyes told me about her shock at this moment.

"Braden Douglas. E. L. Crossley. Third and final attempt on the first height," the event judge called out in a melodramatic way. Even the event judge was having a laugh.

I closed my eyes and prayed. "Please, God. Help me. Get me over this bar."

I gripped the pole with a newfound strength and sprinted down the black asphalt lane toward my nemesis. I planted the pole and jumped with all my might, launching myself forward. I landed on the mat with a thud and looked back. The bar was still up at its height. But the laughter from the crowd revealed the worst. I had flown under the bar and missed it completely. I never made it. I laid on the mats for an extra second, trying to muster up any dignity I had left.

The walk of shame back to the athlete's area past Coach Watkins was horrific. As I passed her, she lifted her large brown clipboard in front of her face, pretending to read the event details of the day. She didn't say a word. She didn't need to.

It was one of the best lessons for me to learn at a young age. I tried to fake it, but I definitely didn't make it. There is no impact or influence on others if you don't make it.

If you're not good at what you do, you'll never become a great leader. Period.

I know that sounds harsh, but a skill that is evident to others and achieves positive results creates credibility. Credibility gives you the right to be heard. The more credible you are, the more powerfully your message will be absorbed by the audience you influence.

For example, I like to play golf, but I'm far from being a pro. During a round of golf with friends, there's bound to be a few people who are better players than me. Sometimes one of them will give me advice on my grip or swing or how to line up a putt. I listen to them a bit but only slightly. But what if Tiger Woods, arguably the best golfer of all time, gives me advice? You better believe I'd listen and do what he says and so would thousands of others.

This breadth and scope of credibility is what is referred to as a platform. The more credible and well known you become in a particular area, the greater your platform, and the broader the impact you can have. CEOs of well-known large companies have a big platform. Celebrities and politicians have big platforms.

To build a platform through your Professional Life, I've come to believe you need the following character traits. There's no specific order but you need these three Ps:

1. Passion
2. Pursuit of excellence
3. Purpose

PASSION

In a professional context, passion is not an emotional high that you have on occasion. Building off the definition from Merriam-Webster's dictionary, passion is an enduring enjoyment that comes from performing or engaging in a skill or activity over an extended period of time.

There will be many things in your life that you're passionate about. Your career. Your family. Faith. Friends. Hobbies or activities. In some cases, your passion for these things can be stronger or weaker as you go through life. However, it's absolutely critical that you have passion in order to have an impact.

There are two components of this definition that I want you to focus on.

The first is the idea of enduring enjoyment. You need to enjoy what you do.

My first real job after my business degree was working at Frito-Lay in marketing. I was a young, ambitious leader who was eager to prove himself. It was the first time I was working with adults of the same age as my parents. Some of these people had been with the company for over thirty years, which was mind boggling to me at the time.

As I said in the introduction, I have a passion for marketing. Building strategies, digging into research, understanding why people buy certain items, and creating new ideas that drive results. I often lose track of time, as I really enjoy it, which sometimes makes my wife mad when she has to call me to tell me to come home.

Have you ever worked with someone who didn't enjoy their profession? Or have you ever received service from someone who didn't find enjoyment in what they did? It's stifling. No one wants to be influenced by them or gravitate to them. If you're not enjoying what you do, change the role or actions, or change the focus to make it enjoyable. This is ultimately what I had to do at Frito-Lay. I needed to change the focus from chips to something I cared about: people.

The second component of passion is about the extended period of time. It's easy to enjoy activities over a short time frame, but enjoyment is only one component of passion. Passion also requires perseverance and commitment to last over a period of time. Your feelings of joy will fluctuate, but passion keeps you going when it gets tough. And if you're doing anything important, there are and will be tough times. I often see people quit jobs too early or give up on an important project or even end a marriage quickly because it gets hard. True passion for something enables you to sustain, and that's what's needed for a great Professional Life.

PURSUIT OF EXCELLENCE

No one follows or is influenced by passion alone. You have to be good. Credibility is earned from achieving positive results over time.

I was playing golf with a friend one day. We were up on a ridge overlooking a par-three hole surrounded by water. It was beautiful.

"If I get a hole in one, I think I'll quit golf," he said.

"Why is that?" I asked, knowing he wasn't really serious.

"Then I would have achieved perfection and could leave while on top," he said.

"I think you're missing the point of golf," I chimed in. "It's a game of mastery and consistency. Anyone can get lucky on a single shot."

He gave me a bit of an eye roll and thanked me for my Confucian wisdom. He went on to hit his ball into the water.

Your Professional Life is a game of mastery and consistency.

The only way to play the professional game well is through the pursuit of excellence. Always learning and always growing. I've tried hard to live this out from an early age.

There was a motivational speaker in my childhood hometown named Bob Koehler. Since my hometown of Fonthill had a population of about eight thousand people, Bob was a rare bird. He would regularly be asked to emcee special events in the community or be the guest speaker at functions.

I went up to him after he spoke at a function in our high school.

"Thanks, Bob, for speaking today. What advice would you give a young person to be successful?" I asked.

I was expecting something along the lines of work hard, enjoy what you do, be considerate, or something along those lines. Instead, he said something that I've never forgotten and have tried to implement in my life ever since.

"Braden, great leaders are great readers," he said.

Bob paraphrased this quote from the thirty-third US president, Harry Truman, who said, "Not all readers are leaders, but all leaders are readers."

Bob was wise. He didn't tell me what to read or how often, but he gave me an insight into what separates leaders from others—the pursuit of excellence. What Bob meant when he said that "great leaders are great readers" is that leaders are always eager to learn. They know they can never know enough, so they read, absorbing as much knowledge and wisdom as they can. They're seeking mastery; they're chasing excellence.

And it matters. Those who pursue excellence through continuous learning become better and more valuable to the people they serve. They gain more credibility, create bigger platforms, and so have more impact. I've witnessed this time and again in my career. The people who are constantly learning, growing, and applying themselves become more valuable and rise faster than others.

How are you learning and pursuing excellence? Do you have a plan for yourself, and are you learning in line with that? And if so, where do you capture your learning? The very rare person has a photographic memory and can recall facts and figures from years of learning. If you're like me, I have so much going on that I need to write things down. I've used journals in the past, but now I use Evernote on my phone. If I'm reading or have an idea or hear something important, I capture it in my notes. Many of the insights and quotes from this book are taken from my notes over the years—knowledge always comes in handy.

If you want your professional life to soar, make sure you're always reading, learning, and capturing. Pursue excellence.

PURPOSE

Have you ever played sports without keeping score? Maybe it was a picnic or just having a fun pickup game. What typically happens? At first, it's usually fun, but after a while, motivation and effort starts to fade. It's amazing what happens when someone mentions, "First to three wins." Everyone seems to get a bit more focused; they push harder and understand what they're playing for now.

Purpose in your Professional Life focuses your passion and provides the motivation to pursue excellence.

Understanding the results of your effort is needed. These results might be a goal, outcome, or compensation that you achieve. It can also be deeper than that and be about people, time with family, or the impact you want to have on others. Obviously, I endorse the latter.

It took me years to dial in my purpose. When someone asked me what I wanted to be when I was young, I knew I needed to sound credible, so I would say professional soccer player, vet (until I realized I hated science), or CEO. The truth was, I didn't know. I just wanted to be important and to be rich. My purpose and focus was all about me. My goals. My dreams. My accomplishments. Sadly, many people still have this view. I was fortunate to learn as a young adult that an abundant and full life was about helping and serving others first.

Helping leaders find true success has been my defining purpose for the past few years. It's written in large letters at my home office to remind me each day. So how do I live it out practically in my business?

To give you a bit of context, I run a large marketing agency named CREW, where we create brands, advertising, and communication focused on the food industry. We run into a lot of gray areas, and this is where your values and true purpose are tested most.

For example, we were approached to create a new brand of a low-cost vodka that was targeted to young men between the ages of nineteen and twenty-four who want to get wasted for less. Should we take it on? If I say no, is marketing wine or craft beer OK? Where do we draw the line? What if we need this client in order to keep our staff employed?

Let's take marijuana and cannabis as another example.

Canada saw a major industry being born when they legalized cannabis. We were inundated with calls from investors that wanted our help to launch and market new brands, retail stores, and equipment for harvesting. Should we help contribute to this new market when weed isn't something I personally want to endorse? We're not breaking any laws, and we could use the profits for good. Is that an acceptable motive? What about CBD, which is found in marijuana but is linked with some great medicinal benefits? Is THC (the hallucinogenic strain in marijuana) bad, but CBD is OK?

What about more macro societal issues? Should we use half-naked beautiful models in product advertising that contribute to the distorted body perception in society? But what if that ad will sell more products for our clients than another idea?

Being ethical and abiding by the laws of a country is the bare minimum. A leader of impact will do that already. Choosing to be a purpose-driven company or leader or executive is what sets you apart. Purpose is subjective and is different for everyone, but you need to create clear guidelines to help you.

At CREW, I started at the very beginning to have a purpose, vision, and values that would make a difference. Our purpose is to be the best marketing agency that builds brands that nourish lives and delight the soul. The vision is to be a global brand for good. And our values are C-R-E-W (Character, Relationships, Execution, and Wow). We then have definitions around each of these, but we also have guidelines for which clients we take on and which ones we don't.

We want to work with clients whose products, services, or organizations make a positive difference in the lives of others.

We don't work with clients that we wouldn't be proud to show on our home page of the website or have our name attached to. I realize this definition is broad, so we created some examples to help each of our leaders make the right decision, and they include the previous examples.

We don't work with products that promote a hard party lifestyle, such as most hard alcohols or cheap beer. Wine is OK. We avoid cannabis and new edibles, as we don't want to market "Bob's Groovy Brownies." However, CBD oil found in cannabis for medicinal benefits is OK. We don't work with clients who have a shady past or bad reputation in the market. We also avoid weird things like witch potions. (Yes, that was a real example.)

We're not perfect, and I've made some mistakes. We've turned down millions in revenue over the past decade, which has hurt us at times. It's especially hard to lay off an employee for lack of work when you turn down revenue that could have kept them with you. But it's in the hard times and difficult decisions that purpose and being a leader of impact becomes real. Remember, impact will cost you.

LEADING ABOVE THE LINE

As my company has grown, we get to hire, train, fire, coach, and develop a lot of employees. It's arguably the main role for a leader as you progress. In the marketing industry, we attract a lot of talented young people, and many of my staff are in the millennial generation. I often hear older leaders quip about "entitled" or "precious" millennials, and I think that's unfair. Yes, they are different and have unique views on purpose and work, not to mention a love of travel and avocados. But they're also passionate and committed and need to be nurtured in what it means to be a leader.

One of the lessons that I believe is important for young leaders, and even older leaders, to understand is the concept of "leading above the line." This is an understanding of how to be a better professional so that you can build more credibility, a larger platform, and achieve greater impact.

This idea came about when a young designer came into my office.

"Braden, I've been here at CREW for over a year, my performance review was strong, and I'd like a larger raise than the small cost of living increase I received," he said.

"I'd love to do that," I said in all genuineness. "How much would you like?"

"Umm, I was thinking seven thousand dollars more per year," he said.

"OK. That's about a 12 percent increase to what you're currently making. Are you giving the company more value and profit to justify that?" I said.

"I'm not sure," he replied.

"Let me show you something," I said as I drew out a simple line graph on the whiteboard in my office.

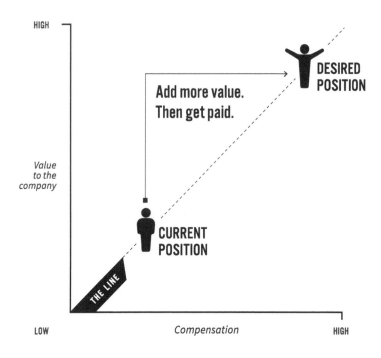

HIGH

DESIRED POSITION

Add more value.
Then get paid.

Value
to the
company

CURRENT POSITION

THE LINE

LOW   Compensation   HIGH

"Your current position was created to bring a specific value and outcome to the company, and you're being paid in line with market rates for this role. Do you agree?" I asked.

"Yes," he said.

"So if you want to make more money, here's what I need from you. Since you've been here for a while, you should be more efficient in completing projects, which means you can take on more work and give us more output. Secondly, as you're someone that people respect in your department, I'd like you to begin teaching the other junior designers how to achieve higher quality and more efficiency. This will give us more profit as a company that I can compensate you with. Are you up for that?" I asked.

"Yes," he said.

"Great. I'll check in with you in the next three months, and if we see results, you can have the raise," I said.

"Awesome. Thank you." He bounced off the chair and back to his desk.

He did achieve the goals and received the raise, and he continues to be a great leader with us.

He understood the principle of leading above the line. If you want to make more money, charge more for products or services, have a greater influence and larger platform, remember this principle: always add value.

Leading above the line is about understanding what brings real value and ensuring you are doing the things that add to it. Building relationships, making connections, coming in earlier, taking initiative, mentoring others, working on projects that help the company in your spare time, and learning new skills that can be applied to get better results in your role are all examples of things you can do to add more value.

This principle can also be applied to people that you want to impact. Add more value in their life. Connect them with others, share advice, encourage them, or give them a new book to read. Understand what they are trying to achieve, take an active interest in it, and add value to it.

You would love for someone to do that in your life. Others will as well. It just takes intention.

KEYS TO REMEMBER

If you want to maximize your Professional Life to make an impact, remember:

- Don't "fake it till you make it." There is no impact or influence on others if you're found to be a fake. Work hard to make it.
- Be passionate. Enjoy what you do and have the commitment and perseverance to keep at it.
- Credibility is essential for a leader, and it's earned from achieving positive results over time. The only way to continuously produce results is with an intentional pursuit of excellence.
- Keep your purpose top of mind.
- Always add value. Whether it's in your job or with others, be the leader who leads above the line and looks for opportunities to add value constantly.
- Remember that the cream always rises to the top. You just need patience in that process.

The path you take professionally is your tool to generate resources. What you do with those resources is your gift to the world.

CHAPTER 6

PERSONAL LIFE

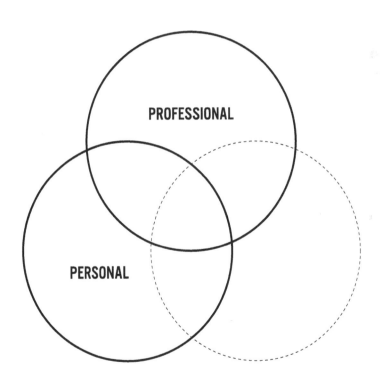

It was my fourteenth birthday, and I was excited. My Uncle Bob and his family were coming over for my birthday dinner. To give you some background, my dad has six brothers and one sister in his family, and Uncle Bob was the oldest brother. He was also the most accomplished in his career and would bring the best presents.

They arrived with a small gift bag that overflowed with white tissue paper and a card popping out of the top. After dinner, the ceremonial cake and birthday song was sung, and it was time to open the gifts. I went for Uncle Bob's first. I opened the card quickly, scanned the contents hoping for money, and went into the gift bag for the kill. Seconds later, I pulled out a book. *The 7 Habits of Highly Effective People* by Stephen Covey.

Wow, I thought to myself. *This gift sucks. Uncle Bob, you really blew this one. I'm a fourteen-year-old active boy who only reads because I'm forced to in school. I might have to start calling you Robert.*

"Thanks, Uncle Bob," I said in a low murmured tone that didn't hide my displeasure.

"Some of the best people I've met in my career all recommend this book," he said. "I thought it could help you."

"Great...great," I repeated as I placed the book on the table.

Days later, my mom eventually moved the book to the night table beside my bed. It sat there for six months. When we would see Uncle Bob and his family at gatherings, such as Easter, he would ask me how the book was.

"Pretty good. Just getting into it," I would say.

July came along, and it was the summer break. I didn't have

a steady job as a fourteen-year-old, so I had a lot of time on my hands. I looked at the *7 Habits* and decided to pick it up. It was the first time I had read a book on personal development.

I'm glad I did.

The second habit that Stephen Covey introduces is "keeping the end in mind." This is the habit of envisioning what people will say about you when you pass away. What will the funeral or memorial for you be like? Who will attend? What legacy will be left?

Even though I was young, thinking about my own funeral had a profound effect on me. Who would truly care if I were gone? What type of son, brother, friend, student, teammate, or neighbor was I? Who did I want to be? How was I going to become that? What type of *impact* would I have?

LIFELINE

An exercise that we do in the first session of LeaderImpact is to plot your life on a line.

BIRTH		DEATH	ETERNITY
YEARS			

What age are you now? How many years do you have left? How are you going to use that time left?

It's a refining exercise as leaders realize two things: (1) there's not a lot of time left and you don't know when it's going to be over, and (2) leaders see how fast time has flown by and what they have done with their life. The whole topic of eternity and what's after death is a whole other section.

But the key insight is that our Personal Lives are finite. There's a beginning and an end. I want to ensure that you keep the end in mind and focus on the relationships that matter and the impact you can have in this world.

IT'S ALL ABOUT RELATIONSHIPS

Some people will tell you that impact in leadership is about the grand actions: building that commercial empire or changing how an industry operates. And those are big and beautiful impacts. But on a more micro scale, at its very essence, impact operates within a perfectly simple subset: relationships.

Let me put it this way. I work with clients in marketing strategy, and we always start with helping the organization understand their purpose. My favorite question to help them think about this is: "If your company disappeared tomorrow, what would be missing? Who would care the most?"

The answer to that question usually comes back to relationships.

The people that would care about the company are the customers you've built a relationship with and who have come to rely on or love your product or service. The employees who trust and rely on you to provide employment. The suppliers who need you to purchase for them. The community at large that the organization is supporting through taxes, gifts, employment, and so on.

Everything we do is interconnected with relationships.

When we think about making an impact as a leader, we always think about the masses. We think about sweeping change and affecting the lives of millions. But impact starts with the relationships closest to you. The people who will take the time to attend your funeral will be those who have or had a relationship with you. The closer the relationship, the closer they will be to your casket when you die. Sobering, I know. But true. Typically, it's immediate family, then extended family, and then close friends, and it trickles out to the back row, where loose acquaintances or colleagues from the past might be.

Remember this: impact in your Personal Life always starts with the relationships you have been given. Sadly, we are sometimes better and more intentional at impacting the "back rows" than the "front rows." When you think about having an impact, I don't want you to think about having an impact on the masses. Think about your closest relationships first. Here's where you have the power to make the most difference every single day.

EXCELLING IN YOUR RELATIONSHIPS

The great basketball coach Pat Riley said, "A team becomes great when each player knows their role, accepts their role, and excels at their role." Your impact becomes great when you know and accept the role you have in your relationships. Choosing which relationships to excel in is one of the greatest choices you'll make. The reason it's the greatest choice is because the greatest and longest-lasting impact will come from these people.

Think about the roles you have in life. Which ones do you play and which are most important to you? Take the time to make a list.

IMMEDIATE FAMILY

- Spouse or partner
- Parent or guardian

EXTENDED FAMILY

- Son or daughter
- Brother or sister
- Aunt, uncle, cousin, nephew, or niece

PROFESSIONAL

- Employee
- Manager, boss, leader, or mentor
- Colleague or associate
- Customer or client
- Supplier
- Competitor

SOCIAL

- Friend
- Teammate
- Neighbor
- Congregant, participant, or attendee
- Student
- Other

Think about the number of people that your role interacts with and the relationships you have with each of these roles. Write down some of the names of these people beside each role. Now, look over this list. Picture the faces of these people. Do you see them? Do you know them? What type of impact could you have in their life?

Before reading this book, if someone asked you what relationships were most important to you, you would probably say the "right" answers. My family, friends, work, and so on. However, I'm a marketing expert, and I know people lie. What we say and what we actually do don't always line up. If you want to know what relationships are most important to you, look at your calendar and bank account, and observe where you spend your time and money.

I believe one of the main reasons leaders fail to live up to their potential for having impact is a misalignment between our relationships and how we spend our time and money. If you want a great marriage but don't spend time together or go out on dates or weekends away, your marriage won't be great. The same is for your kids or family or friends. Where you spend your time, attention, and finances is where growth will be. For many leaders, they invest a lot of time and money into work, and guess what? That's where they find success.

No one usually does this on purpose. It's shrouded in good intentions of providing for your family or sacrificing in the short-term to enjoy more in the long-term. In reality, it's a lack of discipline around time and unchecked self-centeredness. We're committed to the wrong things. We're busy. We're focused in the wrong areas. We just let time fly by and then justify our actions and behaviors.

But we can change that.

FOCUS ON THE RIGHT RELATIONSHIPS

Which relationships are most important? It starts with your immediate family. If you have chosen to get married or be in a committed, lifelong relationship as a partner, this is your top relationship. They will keep you focused on the right purpose, they'll help you check your priorities, they'll motivate you when your passion is fading, and they'll keep you pursuing excellence. You'll also do the same for them. They may not always communicate in the best ways, but that's a whole other book.

When I first married my wife, Jen, she was a great teacher and loved her career. She would be marking papers while we watched a movie on weekends and ask me advice about her class and colleagues. However, when I started the business and we had our first child, her purpose as a teacher changed. Our purpose together changed, and we needed to figure out how to ensure we both were united in this new season. She didn't feel teaching in schools was going to work, but she also didn't feel fulfilled as a stay-at-home mom. It was easy for me, as I was focused on the business, but I knew I had a responsibility to help her, engage with her, and see how she could utilize her gifts. This journey took years, but now she's started a blog for women married to entrepreneurs called TheEntrepreneurWife.com (yes, I just plugged her blog), and she teaches several Bible studies for women. She loves it. And she's good at it.

If you're a parent, this is your next most important relationship. This role and your relationship with your children have seasons when there are heavy commitments and sacrifices in the early years as you care for them and teach them. As they grow, their needs change, and you become a supportive guide, a confidante, and a role model for them to follow. When they leave your home (hopefully not too late), the influential role remains, but the time (and money) is reduced.

Extended family comes next. Communicating, encouraging, being there for events and get-togethers are key. However, just showing up to the lovely Easter dinner is not the same as making an impact. Be intentional in your family members' lives, their dreams, and their purposes, and see where and how you add value. Your family connection creates a bond that gives you permission to care more for them.

Relationships at work are usually more important than people give them credit for. You spend a lot of time with these people and have a direct or indirect influence over them. How are you intentionally building into their lives and caring for them?

Finally, social relationships. Friends, neighbors, teammates, attendees, churchgoers, social club people—the list of people you interact with on a daily and weekly basis is enormous. What role do you have to play with those people? Who do you focus on?

A good reflection exercise is to create a list of the relationships you have that you feel you could impact. You'll notice that the list can be very long. I've created a small sample below of the people and relationships currently in my life.

THEIR RELATIONSHIP WITH ME	NAME	WHAT IS THEIR PURPOSE? GOALS?	WHAT'S ONE THING I CAN DO TO HELP?
Spouse	Jen	Teaching and encouraging women to be successful spiritually and at home	Enable time, money, and effort to help her pursue these activities.
Son	Rylan	Athlete, designer, and intelligent leader	Teach, encourage, and provide opportunities in these areas.
Daughter	London	Speaking, teaching, and leading groups of people	Teach, encourage, and provide opportunities in these areas.
Parents	Dad and Mom	Continue to be purposeful in retirement by helping those in need	Take an active interest in their volunteer activities. Weekly check-in.
Sibling	Marnie	Establishing a new purpose with a young family, new career, and new country	Be engaged and active in her next steps. Weekly check-in.
Boss	Nate	Becoming a national leader for CREW and a person of impact	Formal leadership development training and LeaderImpact involvement.
Boss	Josh	Influencing people to find a deeper purpose	Coach, plan, and help provide avenues for him to share.
Boss	Gerald	Becoming a great creative leader in Canada and with his family	Provide opportunities and avenues to be recognized for the work he and the team are doing.
Friend	Stu	Have impact in the lives of others at home, through Tribe, in his mastermind, and charity	Encourage, engage, and connect him with opportunities. Be a good board member for Village Impact.
Friend	Fredrick	Run a family business well while using his gifts to build God's kingdom	Encourage, be available, and connect him with opportunities.
Friend	Adam	Excel at being an entrepreneur and spiritual leader	Encourage, provide practical help in his business, and connect him with opportunities.

What did you notice about my list? Which part were you most curious about?

I found this exercise hard. Even though I'm writing a book on impact, actually doing it with intention is still hard work. After my spouse and kids, the list of relationships was starting to get out of control. You can't possibly be intentional one-on-one with everyone you know.

I also realized that I didn't know their purpose offhand. I had to ask, dig it out, and create it for them. It seems like it should be an easy task, but it's difficult. Creating the next step or one thing I can do to help forced me to think about practical solutions. Even as I look over the list, I'm still asking: What does "encouragement" really mean? What "opportunities" am I going to connect them with? Take your time with this exercise. It's hard work. And don't be nervous if you find yourself confused about what actions to take. Clarity will come. The point is to refocus you on the relationships that matter, be intentional about the time you're giving them, and continue to be focused about the impact you're making. This is an ongoing discipline, so don't worry if it takes more time.

ONE-TO-ONE AND ONE-TO-MANY

There are so many relationships you could have in your life and only so much time. How can you foster, stay connected, and have impact on more people you care about? One technique I've found to be helpful for me is compartmentalizing relationships to one-to-one and one-to-many. In my closest relationships, I would strive for one-to-one connection. Spending time with them, being intentional, and so on. For others in my life, such as colleagues, larger extended family, and people I've met at speaking events, I can use one-to-many avenues and channels of communication. Social media, this book, speaking at events, writing blogs, and meeting in small groups with LeaderImpact is where I choose to communicate, influence, and help with more than one person. Connect these channels and communication to your purpose to ensure your message is authentic and about them, not you.

FINDING THE RIGHT RESOURCES

Simply focusing on the right roles and relationships is not enough. To truly make an impact, you must have the *resources* to connect with people and impact them. This doesn't just mean money alone but includes the resources of time, focus, and energy that it takes. You must take care of yourself.

There are three components to consider to help you focus your resources to make an impact in your Personal Life:

1. Commit to less
2. Be full of energy
3. Make time

COMMIT TO LESS

In order to have relationships that will lead to impact, you need time and intention. There is no way to do this well if you are stretched too thin. As you went through the list of roles and relationships, what did you notice? There are a lot of roles you play and a lot of relationships. It's overwhelming.

My brother-in-law Josh lives in Kelowna, British Columbia, and he runs one our CREW offices. He's an extreme extrovert, loves people, and gets involved in everything. Within a year of moving to Kelowna, he started up a CREW office, was involved in four business groups, volunteered with his church, engaged in a personal coaching program, sat on the board for a community homeless shelter association, and was a mentor with the Tech Accelerator Program. On top of this, he had two kids under the age of five at home. It was too much, but he felt he had to do all these things to network, make connections, and give back.

"Braden, I think I'm stretched too thin," he said to me.

"You think?" I replied. "How are your most important relationships?" I asked.

"OK, but not great," he confessed.

"Then you need to commit to less and learn to say no," I said.

In Greg McKeown's book *Essentialism*, he tells leaders to learn the power of a graceful no.[4] You are saying no to some good things so that you can say yes to the great things that matter. In a short time, Josh was able to say no to the groups and clubs that were taking up his time and able to find others to fill the void of a few of his volunteer activities. And the results remained the same and even improved for him.

Remember, relationships have seasons, and what you say no to at this time may change in a few years. Saying no doesn't mean forever; it just means for right now.

There are two times a year that I assess my commitments and relationships to ensure I don't overextend myself: New Year's and Labor Day Weekend. I use these two times of the year to evaluate the things I'm involved in. If they are not contributing to the relationships I care about or the impact I want to have, I simply give them a graceful no.

BE FULL OF ENERGY

Energy is the fuel for your machine. Without energy, you're not much use to people or the relationships you want to foster. There's a popular belief or bravado among leaders that they can work hard, be more effective on less sleep, and skip meals all in the name of more effectiveness and productivity. That's simply not true. They may be able to do this for a very short stint, but it will catch up to them. They'll get sick, burn out, or become depressed, which will hurt even more than the small gain they thought they were getting.

You are the only one who can have the impact you want. You must take care of yourself.

According to an article by *Business Insider*, salaries peak at forty-eight years old, life satisfaction peaks at sixty-nine, and psychological well-being at eighty-two.[5] Interestingly, your later years, from fifty on, is also when most people choose to retire, exit the business world, or can't perform because of health reasons. The lifestyle you lived in your twenties, thirties, or forties will catch up with you as you age.

It's a shame when great people just don't have the energy to perform or take care of their grandchildren or utilize all their wisdom and connections as they move into their senior years. They have so much to offer. It's like a pure refreshing water well that has lost the bucket and rope.

If you want to have more energy, it's very basic.

- **Eat well.** We're constantly inundated with diet information. We all know someone who is plant-based, on keto, trying intermittent fasting, reducing sugar, on weight watchers, or whatever the fad diet is moving. Here's what I do. I choose water as my drink of choice. I don't drink alcohol. I eat mainly vegetarian. I choose smaller portions at mealtimes, but I also have a sweet tooth and love to eat desserts. I've come to believe that moderation and being disciplined most of the time has worked well. The idea is to be intentional and keep trying your best. It also helps to have support of friends and family, as it can be tough to be disciplined if you're surrounded by people who don't share your same focus.

- **Sleep to recover.** Sleep is essential, and your body and brain need it to recover. According to the Mayo Clinic, healthy adults need seven to nine hours of sleep per night.[6] At the Division of Sleep Medicine at Harvard Medical School, scientists have uncovered that sleep plays a critical role in immune function, metabolism, memory, learning, and vital functions.[7] There's nothing heroic about pulling late nights working and robbing yourself of sleep. In the internal LeaderImpact survey that was conducted internally to over 500 leaders from the around the world, 55 percent of the respondents had adequate to poor sleep (less than six to seven hours). You end up paying for a lack of sleep with poor performance or becoming sick. When it comes to your body, play the long game.

- **Enjoy exercise.** We all know we need to exercise, but many of us don't get enough of it. Exercise can be a chore for many people. It's hard to find the time in busy schedules or to motivate yourself. The benefits of exercise are enormous. It controls weight, is excellent at preventing diseases—especially those that are heart related—improves mood and fights anxiety and depression, is linked to helping you have a better sex life, and, most importantly, boosts your energy. A good goal is to be active at least five days a week, but make it fun. Combine time with your spouse with exercise. Go for a walk together, swim, or take tennis lessons. Pick up a sport again with friends. I took fifteen years off from playing soccer but picked it up again with a group of men, and it's been great physically and socially. Take up running or road cycling, which is now the new golf. You might even enjoy being in Lycra shorts. As Nike's famous tagline encourages, "Just do it."

· **Smile.** This might sound bizarre, but hear me out. In an article by Dr. Earlexia Norwood, smiling helps our bodies release cortisol and endorphins that reduce blood pressure, increase endurance, reduce pain, reduce stress, and boost our immune systems.[8] People who smile are more approachable, which helps build relationships that, in turn, are used to influence and impact others. If you want to be a leader who has an impact, be someone who smiles. A positive disposition creates more energy.

MAKE TIME

Bill Gates is a master of time management and is never late to meetings. As he says about time, "It's the only thing I can't buy more of." I work in an industry that requires me to track my time. I have every fifteen or thirty minutes planned for every day of the week—yes, every day including weekends. There are larger chunks blocked out on the weekends, such as snowboarding or family game night, but the discipline is engrained. I also leave time in the margins or areas of time that I block as unplanned, but it's rare. Time is one big area in my life I'm a control freak about. We don't know how much we have left, and I want to ensure I maximize it.

Depending on your level of leadership and the size of organizations you are leading, there is never enough time. Your days are full of meetings, more people want your attention on items, and there are many decisions to make. Knowing what meetings or projects or priorities are more important is a difficult task, which is why controlling your time is so important and why you can't afford to waste it or have others waste it. Here are four keys I and other leaders I know use to help manage time:

- **Get up early.** The early mornings before anyone is awake is your time. I wake up at 5:30 a.m. on most mornings during the week. This is a great opportunity to exercise, plan your day, write, and in my case, pray and read the Bible. Most of the successful leaders I know are morning people and get up even earlier. This does mean I go to bed at 10 p.m. because sleep is key.
- **Schedule everything.** Like I've said before, become a master at scheduling everything. Yes, everything. You are the captain of your calendar, and time is your resource. Take charge of ensuring everything in there is important. Every Sunday evening, I scan my calendar, review my priorities and scorecard from the company, and plan out the week. I want to ensure that I'm not distracted with meetings or activities that are not necessary or that could be delegated to others. There are a lot of things you can do, but it doesn't mean you should do them all.
- **Keep meetings short.** Disciplined organizations and disciplined leaders know how to run and control meet-

ing times. I hate long meetings. Fifteen-minute stand-up meetings or thirty-minute meetings are the norm. Rarely do I have any meetings that last longer than that. In my experience, meetings are like water; they'll take up the amount of space given to them. Make the norm shorter, and if you need more time, extend it. I guarantee you'll find time in your calendar and get more done.

· **Get it done faster.** When you start tracking time and scheduling everything, you'll begin to be faster at tasks. Good leaders who get a lot done work with a sense of urgency and pace. They give their full attention to people but then attack their tasks to get them done well. Send that email immediately when you know you can. Walk a bit quicker. Be clearer with your objectives, expectations, and how much time you have. This might sound a bit over the top, but to be a leader of impact, you can't afford to waste time. One of the most successful sellers of tech companies is Basil Peters. He's a master with time. His company, Strategic Exits, was a client of ours, and our meetings with him last about ten or fifteen minutes when, with other clients, that same meeting would last an hour or more. He's kind but direct. He set the expectation of short, succinct meetings at the beginning of our working relationship. He lets you know how much time he has for the meeting and is very clear and direct with his responses. It's amazing how my team adapted and keeps the time succinct.

DR. DINDI DOES THIS WELL

I first met Dr. Keith Dindi at a LeaderImpact gathering in Manila, Philippines. You couldn't miss him. His huge white smile permeates brightly in any room against his black complexion. Keith is a heart surgeon in Kenya, owns a few businesses in Nairobi, and has been volunteering with Leader-Impact for several years, influencing leaders in his country. He has three children, and his wife, Esther, who is also a physician of internal medicine, is a strong social media influencer with her Doctor Fitness handle. My wife is still in awe of her abs.

As you can imagine, Keith doesn't have a lot of time. When he describes his life to me, I wonder about all my free time I didn't think I had. Between the demands of the hospital, his businesses, volunteer activities, and his family, there's not much time left.

"How do you fit everything in and keep your life on track?" I asked him.

"It's not easy, but I think of three things that help me: elephants, birds, and chameleons," he said.

"What? That's the weirdest answer I've heard on this subject. What do you mean?" I asked.

He started to laugh, but he went on to explain his deep wisdom. "It starts with elephants because they're huge. You can't miss them. When I start my day, I ask myself, 'What's my elephant in the room? What is the one thing I know I need to do, but I don't feel like doing or feels overwhelming?' This is the thing I attack first in the morning because you have the rest and energy to do it.

"The next is birds. Birds are creatures of habit. I have one that sings by my window every morning at 6 a.m. Your daily routines are critical, as they keep your mind, body, and soul running smoothly. My routine is the 6 a.m. wake-up call. I have a morning devotion where I spend time talking to God and reading scripture, I exercise for thirty minutes, and I have an early call with my business managers afterward. I try to keep this routine unless my elephant for the day is so huge, in which case I attend to the elephant.

"The last is chameleons. These lizards adapt to their environment and are ever-changing—it's the most creative creature. I have found creativity and thinking to be a leader's secret weapon. I find I'm most creative late in the night. Before I sleep, I usually write down ideas, thoughts, or creative concepts that come to my mind. This is when I ask myself questions about how I can adapt to the ever-changing world around me or how to motivate my teams better. It's at this time I get inspired or have ideas for my paintings too."

"You actually have time for painting too?" I asked in disbelief.

"Sometimes, but it's not as often as I'd like. We all need creative outlets for our mind and talents," he said. "But it's how I prioritize my elephants, birds, and chameleons that makes the difference."

He continued, "It's all about relationships. My first relationship is with God. In my line of work, God is the one that keeps me grounded and sane. Besides my morning time with him, I find myself whispering prayers throughout the day, and I start every surgical operation with prayer. The next most important relationship is my wife. We share of a lot of common interests together, and because she's a medic, she understands my world and the frustrations I can have in dealing with sick people. My kids are the next most important, and they keep me seriously grounded. To them, I'm just Dad. I love and spoil them more than my wife would like, but I always try to provide and build into my family's talents and purpose. That's where I will make the greatest impact."

Couldn't have said that better myself!

It's refreshing and motivating to be with leaders who understand impact in their Personal Lives. All of us can lead in this area well. It just takes time and attention. You will also see the greatest amount of impact in this area over the course of your life than in any other. It's that important.

KEYS TO REMEMBER

If you want your Personal Life to be strong, you need to excel in your relationships. In order to do that well, you need to remember:

- **Keep the end in mind.** What will your funeral or memorial be like? Who will attend? What legacy will you leave? Have this image fuel your motivation as you become a better person and leader.
- **Time goes by fast and life is short.** No one knows when their time is up, so we better use the opportunities we have been given and invest in the relationships that matter.
- **Focus on the relationships in your life.** Start in your home and permeate out from there with intention, clarity, and action that helps others achieve their purpose.
- **Find the right resources.** You have finite personal resources in time, energy, and attention. It's important that you focus them on the areas that matter.
  - **Commit to less.** It will free you up to be more intentional and effective if you focus.

- ○ **Be full of energy.** Take care of your personal machine with better eating habits, proper sleep, exercise, and smiling. It'll feel good to be good-looking on the inside and out.
  - ○ **Make time.** Time is a finite resource, so become of the captain of your calendar and get up early, schedule everything, make meetings shorter, and pick up the pace. You're not getting younger, and the world needs you to make an impact.
- **Harness your elephants, birds, and chameleons.** Like Dr. Dindi mentioned, tackle your elephant in the room first, establish an effective daily routine like a bird, and find your creative outlet like a chameleon.

Give like my Uncle Bob. Don't give the world something they want; give them what they need that truly makes a difference. This gift is you, your time, and your attention, and it starts with those closest to you.

CHAPTER 7

YOUR EXTERNAL SELF

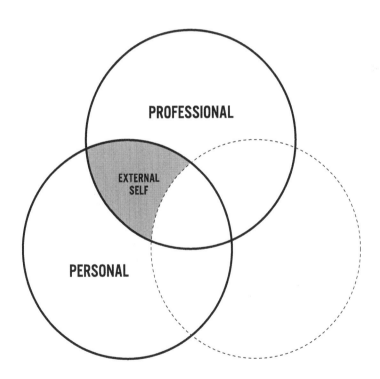

If you combine your Professional Life with your Personal Life, you are looking at your External Self. The External Self is your image. It's what everyone sees and what you want them to. It's how the world perceives you and the identity that you build, protect, or shape. Problems in this area start to occur when who we are is not always what we want others to see.

I grew up in the era when we only had one house phone. I know, the dark ages. It was a monumental moment when we got call waiting. I even remember when my friend got a little box that attached to your phone cord for caller ID. Mind blown. Anyway, when I answered the phone at my house, a lot of callers would think I was my older sister. It was humiliating.

"Hi, is this Marnie?" they would say.

"No, this is not Marnie. It's Braden," I'd respond.

"Oh, I'm sorry. You sound just like your sister," they would say.

There's nothing worse for a preteen boy who already feels uncomfortable with voice cracking to be mistaken as his sister. So for about two years, each time I answered the phone, I would say hello in my deepest possible voice.

Now that I think about it, I sounded ridiculous.

I wish I could say I grew out of this posing phase, but I didn't. I remember putting on the AAA hockey jersey of my best friend, Matt Reid, when I attended a summer hockey camp. He was always bigger than I was, and he gave me a lot of his old equipment and gear that he grew out of. I never made AAA. I was a new kid, and I wanted the players at that summer camp to think I was a better player than what I was. It gave me a bit of swagger as I put it on. It was going well until one of the players from my friend's AAA team came out to the camp one day and noticed me wearing it.

"Hey, Douglas, why are you wearing our jersey?" Busted. That was an awkward moment.

These small things didn't stop with my teenage years either. They carried into my adult life. I was twenty-seven when I started my company, and I was consulting and working with much older adults on their businesses. I look young, too, which will benefit me when I'm seventy, but I saw it as a deficit when I was starting out.

When clients asked, "How old are you anyway?" I would lie.

"Thirty-ish."

As I got older, the age I told them just seemed to increase.

My insecurity drove me to create an impression and desirable image for others. I've matured past this, but I sometimes feel the urge to make myself appear better, especially when I'm in the room with accomplished people.

ALWAYS ON

Managing an ideal image to the world is a skill that leaders develop. Leaders find they are always on. Our days are filled with meetings, requests, and important decisions that need to be made. We have pressures of deadlines, making the deal, selling an asset, paying payroll, and staying ahead of the market or competition. Your employees, suppliers, customers, and families look to you, and you need to seem in control, so you're careful with the words you say and information you divulge. Many leaders find it hard to make friends because they don't have the time or find much in common with others apart from business. Always being on and living up to an image that you want to present to the world is exhausting. What's worse is that it can become such a norm that you forget what it's like to be yourself. This posture and image preservation is why I believe leaders find it difficult to be authentic and vulnerable.

It is extremely evident when I'm leading LeaderImpact groups. I recently started a LeaderImpact group with about fifteen entrepreneurs who meet at our offices every other Friday. Some of them knew each other from various activities in the community, in business, or church, but many were meeting each other for the first time. I open the group by having everyone saying their name, business, and answering the three questions:

- How's your Professional Life (business, work, etc.)?
- How's your Personal Life (family, health, etc.)?
- How's your Spiritual Life (faith—if any—peace, thoughts)?

Without fail, everyone always says they are doing well in all areas of their life. It's amazing. I've been leading groups for almost twelve years, and it's the same every time we start. Even after I mention that confidentiality is a core value of the group and that what is said at the group stays in the group. Everything is still fantastic. I'm either very good at attracting the best leaders, or everyone is distorting the truth to some degree.

I get it. No one wants to be that guy who talks about their issues with a bunch of leaders they only just met. That's awkward. But it reinforces the tendency of leaders to portray an image and uphold it. Leaders want to be known as winners even if they are losing in the moment. However, character development and improvement only comes when we're real, see our own flaws, and are OK when others we trust see them too. This is the reason for the LeaderImpact Assessment. You need to recognize the areas in your life that need to be addressed in order to become a leader of impact.

I have a friend who is a good guy with a great business, and he appeared to have an amazing marriage. Then one day, he announced to me, "Braden, my marriage has been terrible for years, and I'm considering a divorce."

"What?" I said with a stunned look on my face.

"I think it's over," he continued.

Luckily, he and his wife are trying to work it out now. I feel for him. He considered me a close friend but felt so ashamed that he was struggling and didn't want me or others to think he was a failure or had a bad marriage.

Even though this is a leadership book, I want you to forget about being a leader. Focus on becoming a person worth following. As I mentioned in chapter 4, impact is more about *who* you are than *what* you do. A person worth following knows who they are, why they're leading, and they invite and inspire you to do the same.

Pride is at the root of upholding an image and keeps you in the always-on mode. Posturing that is inconsistent with your true self will become more self-centered over time. You will begin to see everything from your own perspective, and you'll care more about what you want, your goals, or your dreams more than others, and that is the opposite of impact.

THE GARDENER AND HORSE BREEDER

One of my favorite stories that reveals unchecked pride is from Tim Keller's book, *The Prodigal God.*[9]

Once upon a time, there was a gardener who grew an enormous carrot. So he came to the palace and said to his king, "My lord, I'm a gardener, and this is the greatest carrot I've ever grown and ever hope to grow. Therefore, I am presenting it to you as a token of my love and respect."

The king was touched and discerned the man's heart. He said, "I have a field that lies next to yours. I will give this field to you so that you can farm it along with your own."

The gardener went home rejoicing.

A nobleman in the court overheard this, and he thought to himself, *A field for a carrot!* So, the next day, he came to the king with a magnificent stallion. "I breed horses," he said, "and this is the finest horse I have ever bred or ever will breed, so I am presenting it to you as a token of my love and respect."

The king discerned his heart and said, "Well, thank you very much."

The nobleman couldn't hide his disappointment.

So the king said, "Let me explain: the gardener was giving me the carrot, but you were giving yourself the horse."

Who are you? The gardener or the horse breeder? The immediate answer and the right answer is the gardener. However, when I read this story a number of years ago, I realized I was a horse breeder dressed up as a gardener.

CHECKING YOUR MOTIVATION

I want people to think that my motivations are pure. That I'm a good guy who cares about them. As I reflect on my life, I did care, but there is an underlying selfishness to ensure that my goals and my dreams were being fulfilled. If I help this person, they in turn will help me. If I'm nice to people and positive, they'll also be nice and help me achieve what I want. It's karmic thinking. If I do good things, good things will come back to me.

The problem with this thinking is that it's all about me. What would happen if good things didn't happen to me? Would I stop being nice, thoughtful, and positive? The gift from my Uncle Bob—the *7 Habits of Highly Successful People*—brought me into the world of self-help. It changed my life. There was a positive momentum that started to occur because I was more self-aware and intentional about my thoughts, behavior, and actions. However, if you only stay in self-awareness, it can have a negative effect as well. Self-help soon becomes all about the self.

Impact is ultimately about others. Not yourself. You should want to help others succeed because it's the right thing to do. Your motivation should not be about the positive outcomes that come from doing the right thing. It should be wanting to do the right thing because you enjoy it. It's intrinsic. There's an understanding of moral truth that you stand for, that you love, that helps you to see others with eyes of compassion and empathy.

Your actions shouldn't be motivated out of duty or strategy to acquire certain outcomes. I've been around smart people who understand the game of influence and try to manipulate outcomes for themselves and the organization. This is the root of politics in an organization. No one believes their intentions are evil. They mean well for the organization, but their intentions are self-focused. They believe their way or strategy is best.

I hired someone who was an emotional strategist. He was on my executive team and was a sharp guy. I didn't know the extent of his strategy until I was meeting with him one day, and he started to talk about how he wanted to get someone in the organization to do what he wanted. He outlined a plan to win this person's confidence, to plant the idea as their own, and to have them be motivated by a promotion to make it happen. To many people, it would have sounded like a fantastic plan. In his mind, he was being a good executive and doing what was best for the company. To me, it screamed of callous manipulation. It placed the needs of the company above people. It also made me realize that I couldn't trust this person. In many organizations, you have to learn to work with people like this, but I don't have to. I let him go, which was expensive. A culture of trust is more important in the long run than short-term results.

CORE BELIEFS

Possessing selfless motivations for the benefit of others is not natural. If you have kids, you'll see firsthand that we are naturally selfish. I still remember my son shoving his baby sister and grabbing a toy she was playing with. This was pretty much a daily occurrence despite our incredible motivational speeches to him.

Motivation is derived from what's important. What's important to you and me is about what we value. Is earning more money worth spending a bit less time at home? Is a larger house worth the extra financial pressure? Is making the deal worth hurting the relationship that might be offended? Is going out with the guys a better option than date night with your wife? These scenarios are not right or wrong. They also don't involve breaking the law or legal issues; they're about what you value. The question you need to ask yourself is: Why do you value something?

The motivation underpinning your values directs your behavior and the decisions you make. Ultimately, what you value originates from your core beliefs. For example, if you believe that life is about getting ahead and maximizing your well-being, you will focus on those outcomes. If you believe you need to live and spend money wisely, you will save, take less risks, and make different decisions than someone who feels money is just a tool to build the best life with. What are your core beliefs? Where did they come from? Are they based on religion, what your parents taught you, or just a collection of beliefs you've gleaned over your life?

My friend Jeremy Laidlaw is a great example of a leader with pure motivations and strong core beliefs. I first met Jeremy in university when he worked in the athletic department, updating, building, and maintaining the athletic department websites. He was also in the business program, and we had a mutual friend, Stu, who was on the varsity soccer team with me. Jeremy is a self-proclaimed nerd. He doesn't hide it or shy away from that title, and what you see is what you get with him. He started his own web and software company shortly after earning his degree and has been pretty successful. However, what really sets him apart are his strong core beliefs. Even in his early twenties, he had a foundation of helping others, speaking the truth, working hard, and being morally upright. He could be a bit uptight and inflexible at times, but you never doubted his intentions, motivation, or character.

No one ever had an issue with Jeremy. He made an impact with people throughout his time at the university that still reverberates there today. Jeremy's core beliefs came from his Christian worldview. I wasn't a Christian in university, but I admired him for being authentic and true to his External Self. He's still the same guy today.

KEYS TO REMEMBER

Managing your External Self is a skill that many leaders and executives have mastered. It can be positive and effective, but it also has a selfish motivation that can be very negative. When thinking of your External Self in the context of impact, remember:

- **What is motivating you?** When you face a situation where you want to embellish, stretch the truth, or make yourself look better, think about what's motivating you. Why do you feel the urge to do this? Is it worth it? It usually never is, and being yourself and authentic will always be better in the long run.

- **Be the carrot farmer.** Be simpler in your approach to people and life and find the joy in what you do. Thinking of others, being generous, and celebrating successes is a great way to build an external identity.
- **Find your core beliefs.** Every word you speak and action you take stems from your core beliefs. If you want more wisdom and if you want your actions to yield better results in your life, examine the beliefs and values that have shaped you. It's a foundation for a lasting identity.

The pressure to perform or project a certain self as a leader can be overwhelming. But I want to remind you that there is no one else in the entire world like you. No one has your abilities, your experiences, your mind, or your relationships. Everything you have accomplished or failed at has brought you to this point in your life. This is who you are. Authenticity matters, motivation matters, giving of yourself—easily and selflessly, like the carrot farmer—matters. There's no need to pretend to be who you are not, even if you are frustrated with where you are right now, for it will only keep getting better. You can and will be a leader of impact. Be secure in the knowledge that you will always be a work in progress, but you can make an impact even with flaws.

> **CHAPTER 8** ⟨

SPIRITUAL LIFE

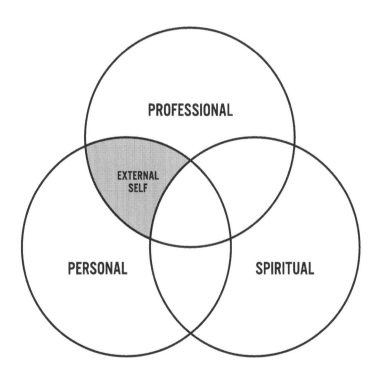

I sat on the side of my bed in my small room staring into the mirror perched on the dresser beside it. I looked at my reflection and saw the tears streaming down my cheeks. This was my wake-up.

"This is not me. What's going on?" I said to myself. "Pull yourself together, Braden." But I couldn't help it. I kept sobbing.

I was recounting the decisions I'd made throughout my life. The drive for good grades, popularity, activities that would look good on a CV, the best program at university that would lead to the best job, and choosing the highest-paying one. The motivation for the vast majority of the things I did was for achievement. To be the best and be someone significant. The best part—I was doing what I set out to do.

And it was shallow. I was a giant living puddle. Have you ever seen and stepped into a giant puddle? They're a mile wide and an inch deep and nobody likes being in it after a while.

I knew a lot of people but didn't have close relationships. My lens for decision-making was always about me and strategizing how each decision was going to help me achieve my goals. Of course, no one knew this true nature of mine, but I did think this way, and it wasn't pretty. I knew I needed a real change. It wasn't just a change of activities or actions or career. I needed a heart change, and I knew it was a spiritual matter.

But I hated church and religion.

I grew up going to church with my parents. The services were extremely boring, I had nothing in common with the kids there, and I felt there was no real upside to faith, except that it gave small-minded people hope that there was something more after they died. My parents were hardcore Christians and always hoped that I would find what they had found.

Now here I was, years later, sitting on my bed, looking at

myself coming apart. I opened the drawer to my night table and reached for the Bible that my mom placed in there when she helped me move in. It was still brand new.

I started to read the book of Luke and look for all the parts that had red lettering. Some Bibles highlight in red when Jesus spoke so you can find his words more easily.

Jesus was doing all these miracles throughout the towns and villages in Israel and teaching people how to know God. Hordes of people would follow him around and want to be with him. He was the ultimate celebrity of the time. But then he does something profound and asks the crowd something that would eventually change my life as well.

If any of you wants to be my follower, you must give up your way, take up your cross, and follow me. If you try to hang on to your life, you lose it. But if you give up your life for my sake, you will save it. And what do you benefit if you gain the whole world but lose your soul? Is anything worth more your soul?[10]

Jesus didn't want the crowds or fame. He never asked anyone to just believe in him either. His focus was on followers.

"Yowza," I called out and threw the Bible on the bed as if it jumped up and bit me. I didn't like reading what Jesus was saying because I wanted my life to be mine alone, but I realized it wasn't anyway.

For the next few days I kept thinking about it. What is a follower? Who am I following? What am I giving my life for?

I needed answers but didn't really want to go to a church.

Today, there are so many resources online to browse and do some research, but back in the early 2000s, there wasn't anything that good. But I did see something that caught my attention. There was a new church in my area called the Meeting House that had some good branding, which as a marketer I liked. But what sold me was their tagline: "A church for people who aren't into church." Perfect—that's me.

For the next few months, I showed up each week. The teaching pastor was a guy named Bruxy Cavey, a long-haired, smart communicator with a sharp sense of humor who loved Star Wars. He reminded me of a chubby version of what I imagined Jesus looked like.

I asked a lot of questions. If I was going to follow a historical figure from two thousand years ago, I better be certain about it. I definitely didn't want to be lumped into the crazy Christian category that I swore I would never be like.

After cutting through the canned answers and clichés, I was finally able to distill the essence of Christianity down to one word: love.

God is love. And his desire is for us to love him and love others.

The stories, rules, and commandments are all designed to help guide us toward a life of love. Jesus's sacrifice on the cross for our sins was love. Meeting with his disciples for the last time before he died, he gave them a final commandment: "Love one another, just as I have loved you. Greater love has no one than this, that one lay down his life for his friends."[11]

Even the Beatles would reinforce this idea that "All You Need

Is Love." Although, I'm sure their definition of it would be different.

At some point, I had to take a chance on love and make a decision to love God and follow Jesus without knowing every single fact or detail. This is why they call it faith. It's about trust.

As I was driving home after hanging out with some of the friends I met at the church, I said out loud, "Jesus, I believe in you. I'm sorry that I've lived for myself all these years. Help me to follow you with my whole life." That was it. Lightning didn't strike the car. I didn't have an out-of-body experience. I just had peace and renewed focus on change. It felt like a new beginning for me, and it started me down a path that would, in fact, change my life.

During an Entrepreneurial Leaders Organization conference in Winnipeg, Ray Pennings, the Executive Vice President of the Cardus Group, presented the results of a 2019 religious study that his firm and the research firm, Angus Reid, had commissioned in 2019. In this study, they found 67 percent of Canadian adults believe God is real. But only 16 percent attend a religious service (aka church), and only 14 percent read a religious text (aka the Bible). My hunch is that these stats would be similar around the world, especially in places with a British or European colonial history. This tells me that people like the idea of God, and they might even like the teachings of Jesus, but they're not following him.

I don't know where you stand on this topic of God and Jesus, but I personally believe it's important to understand, as it relates to impact.

WHY IS A SPIRITUAL LIFE IMPORTANT FOR IMPACT?

Everyone has a Spiritual Life. This is what you believe and what you value. For many people, their Spiritual Life is connected to a higher power or religion. Others grew up in a nonreligious home and instead use laws and rules of their society to be their spiritual guide. Many people I talk with today have a mixture of beliefs, like a moral cocktail, that is unique to them and fits with the life they want. A spiritual life defines morality and has defined moral laws for societies over thousands of years.

Hear me out. You don't need to be a religious person or be devoted to God in order to have impact. There are examples of good leaders that have had a lasting impact on others without a religious Spiritual Life. However, I think those leaders who make an impact without a defined Spiritual Life are rare. The world needs more leaders of impact. A strong Spiritual Life grounded on a tried-and-true foundation that is connected back to the creator of the universe, who is love, is a pretty solid basis to start a movement that will change the world.

On the surface and in our consumeristic culture, the moral cocktail approach to a Spiritual Life and living by laws seems ideal. But who determines what is morally right and wrong? What's right for you may not be right for me, so where do we create common ground?

In democratic countries, the party with the most votes decides the laws. Is the majority of people always right? Are you going to base your beliefs on a collective of people who happened to be voted into power because of their popularity in a small region?

What about forgiveness? Can you legislate that all people must forgive others? We intrinsically know that the benefits of forgiveness are powerful for people in restoring relationships and to achieve harmony with others. Restoration as a whole is critical for society at large, but we can't force people to forgive others. I try to force my kids to forgive each other after a fight—I can tell when they're sincere and when they're not.

What about greed or selfishness? Can we legislate your desire for more? Most economies are built on consuming and acquiring things we want. How you determine what you need is going to be different than someone else.

What about helping others and being generous? Can you force people to have pure motives to help others or give their hard-earned money away? Is compassion something that can be made into a law?

The right Spiritual Life is not about rules to follow. Some people believe that if they follow all the rules and are good people, God will bless them, and their life will be good. That's not true to God's character. God loves you, and he wants you to love and respect him in return. If you love him and believe that he has your best interests at heart, you'll do what he asks. Think about it this way: I love my kids, and I love to spend time with them. I also have rules that help protect them, which they may not understand or always agree with. One of our rules is: "Work before play." Our kids have to do their chores or homework before they can play with their friends or get on their phone. They hate this rule. But I hope my kids don't just follow this rule out of fear of punishment or because they want something from me. I hope they love me and obey this rule because they trust that I know what's best for them. They may not see it until they're much older and more mature, but their obedience is a trust factor based on love.

Jesus says the greatest commandment in the Bible is "to love God with all your heart, all your soul, and all your mind."[12] And the second greatest commandment is equally important: "Love your neighbor as yourself."[13] You'll notice that these are heart issues. Do you really love God and love others? Many leaders have a hard time surrendering what they want to follow God. I get it. It's hard. But when you do, your heart will change. You will become a new person and continue to be refined over time. Your new self will be more caring, compassionate, forgiving, and gracious with others. This heart posture is what's needed in order to become a leader of impact.

DO YOUR OWN RESEARCH

There are people reading this book who don't believe in God or won't, and that's OK. All I ask is that you do the research and understand why you're making that decision. If you keep searching and asking and being open, you will find the answers. As a leader, you're smart enough to make one of the most important decisions of your life. Just don't shrug it off or be close-minded.

I was with a leader who told me that he didn't believe in God because he didn't like the Christians in his hometown. He thought they were fake, and the worst entrepreneurs he does business with are Christians too. It's true. There are a lot of people who call themselves Christians but don't live it out well. Many can be bigots, short-sighted, unintelligent, or mean-spirited, but that doesn't change who God is.

There are a lot of people who claim to be soccer players, but when you see them play, it's obvious: they're terrible at it. It doesn't mean soccer is a bad sport and you shouldn't play; it just means these people are a bad representation of the real thing. The same is true of Christians. Just because they might be terrible at it doesn't mean God is not worth it.

EVIDENCE OF A STRONG SPIRITUAL LIFE

Paul of Tarsus was the first Christian to take the message of Jesus to people other than the Jews. Most of the New Testament in the Bible was written by Paul as he was instructing and helping these new Christians live a strong Spiritual Life. He tells them through a letter to the Christians in Galatia (modern-day Turkey) that you will know if you have a strong Spiritual Life if these eight qualities are present in your life.

1. Love
2. Joy
3. Peace
4. Patience
5. Kindness
6. Goodness
7. Gentleness
8. Self-Control

These characteristics are more commonly known as the "fruit of the spirit."[14] Just as you know a good apple tree by the taste, size, and beauty of its apples, you can know your Spiritual Life by these characteristics in your life.

Does your life produce this type of fruit?

LOVE

Love has so many meanings with so many cultures. It's defined as an intense feeling of deep affection. You can say you love someone, but it's really shown in action. In another letter to Christians, Paul had needed to explain what love is to help people understand how to be someone who loves.

> Love is patient and kind. Love is not jealous or boastful or proud or rude. It does not demand its own way. It is not irritable, and it keeps no record of being wronged. It does not rejoice about injustice but rejoices whenever the truth wins out. Love never gives up, never loses faith, is always hopeful, and endures through every circumstance.[15]

This passage is often read at weddings, but I believe it extends far beyond a marriage. It's a recipe for life. Jesus even said to his disciples that the world will know you are my followers by the way you love each other. How are you showing love in your life?

JOY

Joy is defined as a feeling of great pleasure and happiness, but I think that definition is limited to an emotion. Chasing after emotions is like trying to get rich. When do you know you've achieved it? In the leader assessment, 75 percent of respondents expressed they wanted to experience more joy in their life. That's a high number, but again, it's probably based on the varying definitions that exist about what joy is.

I believe joy is a confident assurance of a positive outcome. If you're a Christian, you know that you're going to be in heaven one day. You've won an amazing prize that you didn't even deserve. It was a free gift because of what Jesus gave—his life. That understanding should fill you with positive emotion that lasts. This is why joy shouldn't change with circumstances. You can still be a joyful person and sad over present circumstance at the same time. As a leader, people like being around others who are joyful. It's an attracting quality and is needed in times of crisis, loss, pandemics, and hardships. Joy lifts the spirits of others. What leader doesn't want to be known for that?

PEACE

Paul was a Hebrew, and his understanding of peace was different than the modern or Western worldview. We view peace as the absence of conflict. However, to Paul, peace or "shalom" means to be safe in mind, body, or estate, which is why "shalom" has been used as a salutation. Its underlying meaning is to capture a sense of wholeness or completeness. In this definition, you would have an absence of conflict, but you'd also have much more that would prevent conflicts from occurring.

As a leader, you set the tone in your work culture and home. Is there a sense of peace (wholeness, completeness, contentment) in the places where your leadership is present? This environment enables better decision-making with an absence of politics and vain distraction. Would others sense a wholeness and peace in your life or leadership?

PATIENCE

I'm obsessed with time, and I'm goal-oriented, so the character trait of patience has been a hard one for me. It's probably difficult for a lot of leaders, especially the type-A ones. I want to give you a new perspective on patience that I think will help as you become a leader of impact.

Patience is not being idle. It's not waiting around being unproductive or accepting poor performance. Patience is your capacity to accept or tolerate delay or suffering without becoming angry or upset. It's an endurance character trait. Why is this important as a leader? Because people and circumstances will not always work or abide with your timelines or expectations. They will disappoint you. How you respond will make all the difference.

I hired a new marketing manager who I felt wasn't getting it. They would constantly ask questions, and their work was only average. On top of this, I was busy. I was becoming frustrated, and one day, when she came in to ask me another question, I lost my patience. She left my office in tears. This does not help build a positive culture that endures. I felt terrible and called her into my office later that day. She reluctantly came in and plunked herself in the chair ready for round two.

"I'm sorry," I started. "I should never have lost my patience, and I hurt you in the process. Can you forgive me?" I said. "How can I help you perform so that you and I both can see the results?"

She did forgive me (thankfully). And she went on to explain how our lack of training and onboarding process really set her back. She was right. I was expecting her to just know how everything worked and what was expected without the proper upfront training. Since then, she's turned into a great employee, and we have a better onboarding and training process in place because of it. My lack of patience almost cost me a great employee.

How are you at accepting or tolerating delay or suffering?

KINDNESS

It's the quality of being friendly, generous, and considerate toward others. A strong Spiritual Life will give you a heart that wants to help others. You don't give out of guilt or expecting something in return. You give because you're a kind person, and that's what you do. Leaders who make an impact are kindhearted, and they take the time to invest in others because they care.

Having worked with hundreds of leaders, I've found the leaders who are kind have a better understanding and insight into their customers and consumers than those who don't. The kind leaders are then able to make better product decisions, launch more successful campaigns, and even recruit better employees, as they foster trust easier. Kindness matters.

Would the people who know you best describe you as kind?

GOODNESS

Goodness is being committed to doing what is morally right. It's choosing good over evil. If you are a Christian, it's following the commandments of God, not out of duty but because you love him and want to glorify him. If you don't follow a specific religion, it could mean pursuing ethical and moral standards.

As a leader, you are faced with key decisions every day, and a leader of impact ensures their decisions are always above board. Whether establishing contracts, paying taxes, reporting results, communicating with customers and employees—or the number of other issues you deal with—leaders with the quality of goodness always do the right thing.

Are you operating with goodness in every aspect of your life?

GENTLENESS

At first glance, gentleness and leadership don't seem to mix. The term *gentleness* gives me mental images of soft-spoken people who are physically weak and quiet. That doesn't seem like a leader I'd like to be. This image is not what Paul intended when he wrote this to the Christians in Galatia who would be facing a lot of persecution from others for their faith. Gentleness is the ability to stay humble and compassionate toward the struggles or shortcomings of others.

Gentleness as a leader is hard. Leaders are usually gifted in certain areas, they operate at a higher capacity, and they may have a higher drive or IQ as well—so how do they deal with people who are not at their level? Do they look down on them? Does the leader feel superior to others? Gentleness is about how you handle and work with others, especially those who are not as strong as you in certain areas. Your view toward employees and how you treat suppliers is a very good indication of this character trait in your life. Even if you get results from a surly or domineering approach, that doesn't make it right. Results are only a small piece that matters. Impact is what you should be striving for. Would the people under your influence or who deal with you view you as gentle and humble?

SELF-CONTROL

Paul gives this character trait last. It's the final eight ball on the table. Why does he do that? I think it's because self-control is the oil that enables you to keep the other character traits going. Self-control is being the master of your emotions, desires, and behavior. Love, joy, peace, patience, kindness, goodness, and gentleness all require you to be intentional and to act. Intentions are easy, but putting those actions into practice, or restraining yourself, takes control.

I was driving along the road back to our house after work when the temperature outside dropped. I was in total control of the car until I hit ice. The car was moving toward a ditch, and my stomach dropped. Even though I pumped the brakes or turned the wheel, there was nothing I could do. Luckily, I stopped just as the front of the car peered over the edge of the ditch.

Being out of control with your emotions, thoughts, or behaviors will eventually put your life in a ditch. How many leaders do you know who have ruined a deal, contract, employee, or business because they didn't exercise control in one of these character traits? Unfortunately, I know many, and it's too bad, because it didn't need to be that way for them. Self-control, just like these other traits, can be worked on. You can improve and keep making these traits a bigger part of your character and Spiritual Life.

How is your level of self-control?

STAY CONNECTED

These eight character traits would benefit a leader immensely, and we should want to see these traits alive and well in all of us.

However, we can't strive to attain them in our own strength. If you're a leader, you have a great work ethic and probably more capacity to perform than others. When you see a list of traits that could help you, you naturally want to start working on them and bring them into fruition. But you need to be careful with the motivations behind these traits.

Jesus addressed this very issue on the night before his death. He was having dinner with his disciples (aka "The Last Supper"), and he said to them, "I am the vine; you are the branches. Those who remain in me, and I in them, will produce much fruit. For apart from me you can do nothing."[16]

What does he mean that "apart from me you can do nothing"? There are countless people doing a lot of good things with these traits who don't believe or follow Jesus. So what is Jesus saying?

Jesus was preparing these disciples to be leaders in a new movement. They would be serving people. Sacrificing themselves for the greater good. They would face torture and persecution. But they would also see and perform miracles. Crowds of people would flock to them and hail them as great leaders. People would offer them money in exchange for God's power. These disciples would need to have these traits in order to lead well, but they would need to be anchored spiritually in a relationship with Jesus, or it would be in vain.

That is Jesus's point and the reason a strong Spiritual Life, rooted with him, is needed for leaders of impact.

A BORN REBEL

Lorne is a friend of mine, a great leader, and president of a successful communications company with retail chains, corporate sales, repair, and accessories. He has a strong humble disposition and deep Spiritual Life, but he wasn't always that way.

"My life was a mess. I didn't have a spiritual life in my teens and early twenties, and I was doing whatever I felt like doing. Soon, my drinking and partying lifestyle had me hanging out with the wrong crowd," he said. "In my early twenties, I got into trouble with the law, and it cost me a fortune in lawyer fees just to keep myself out of prison."

"What happened? How did you turn it around?" I asked him in disbelief.

"A girl," he said with a smile. "I was dating Ingrid, and I wanted her to move in with me."

"Not a chance," she told him. "We need to be married in a church, or else we're breaking up."

"There's no way a pastor is going to marry us. Not with my past," Lorne responded.

He loved Ingrid. He finally found a distant relative that would marry them in February. However, soon after they were married, Lorne realized marriage was not the solution to his problems. He was still drinking too much and working even harder in the business.

"I knew my marriage would be over in a hurry if I didn't

change," he said. "I was also sick and tired of looking over my shoulder when I was out in public for the damage I had done in other people's lives," he continued.

That September, the pastor who married them came over to Lorne's house to check up on him and Ingrid. After a short visit, the pastor shared that God still loved Lorne and had a plan for his life. Lorne just needed to come to God and ask for forgiveness and start following him. It was that easy. That afternoon, Lorne and Ingrid both decided to believe in Jesus and follow God wholeheartedly.

"It wasn't easy. We told our friends and lost those relationships, which was tough even though we knew those relationships were unhealthy. I also tried to make amends with the people I had hurt in the past. That was challenging and humbling. Even though choosing God wasn't easy, it's worth it," Lorne said. "I have a peace and foundation to my life that is better than anything I could ask for."

Lorne and Ingrid have been happily married since and have four children and eleven grandchildren today. He continues to lead LeaderImpact groups in his city and mentors leaders one-on-one. He firmly believes a strong Spiritual Life is critical to having an impact because it helps you understand that leadership is not about you and that being transparent and honest is always the right decision even if it ends up costing you.

His advice to leaders is to make a straight path toward the finish line in your life. Close every door and say no to anything that takes you off this path of doing what is right and living with integrity.

A strong Spiritual Life and being with others who keep you accountable will enable you to do this.

KEYS TO REMEMBER

Everyone has a Spiritual Life, which creates the foundation for your values, thoughts, and actions. At LeaderImpact, we believe that in order to be a leader who makes a lasting impact, your Spiritual Life needs to be grounded in a love for God and being a follower of Jesus. This is where the selflessness and power to serve comes from. To help you along this path, remember:

- **Do the research.** Understand who God is and why Jesus is so important. If you keep searching and asking and being open, you will find the answers. You're a leader, and you're smart enough to make one of the most important decisions of your life. Just don't shrug it off or be close-minded. God is patient and waiting for you.
- **Work on your "fruits of the spirit."** The character traits that Paul laid out give us a great standard to strive for. Take an inventory of how you're doing in those areas, and answer the questions I ask after each trait. Keep working on them and improving. They all work together to create a great fruit salad of leadership that people rave about.
- **Practice the Golden Rule.** Many of us know the Golden Rule: "Do to others as you would have them do to you." If you practice this rule in your life and make decisions by it, you'll be far ahead as a leader who makes an impact. Isadore Sharp instituted the Golden Rule as the main core value of the Four Seasons Luxury Hotel chain and used it as the foundation for their remarkable culture of service. It can be the same for you, your company, and your life.

The apostle Paul states that we all need faith, hope, and love, but the greatest one is love. A leader who has impact is ultimately in the business of loving others. To do this, we need a strong Spiritual Life. Making your Spiritual Life part of your identity starts in your Internal Self.

CHAPTER 9

YOUR INTERNAL SELF (PERSONAL AND SPIRITUAL LIFE)

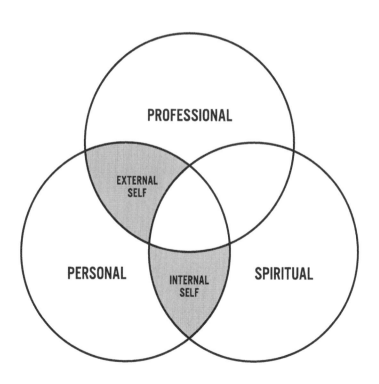

It was 1988. I was in fourth grade, out riding my bike on the neighborhood streets with two of my friends. It happened to be spring cleaning time, and neighbors were clearing out garages and leaving their used goods on the streets to be picked up by the city trucks the next morning. As we were riding by, an older couple carrying boxes out of their garage waved us over.

The woman was in jeans and wearing a baggy red sweater; she dropped a big box in front of us.

"Our son has long been out of the house, and we're clearing out his stuff," she said. "He has all these hockey cards. Do you boys want them?"

We didn't need to think twice about it. "Yes!" we shouted (probably in unison) and proceeded to jump off our bikes and race over to the newly found treasure that had—by some wonderful twist of fate—found its way to us.

Talk about hitting the jackpot. The hockey cards were from the 1960s, 70s, and 80s, and were in pretty good condition. We separated them into three piles, making sure they were all even by height. (Hey, when you're nine, that's your benchmark.)

There were all kinds of cards with the big names in hockey: Bobby Orr, Gordie Howe, Frank Mahovlich, and Phil Esposito. In my stack, though, was a 1979 O-Pee-Chee Wayne Gretzky rookie card. I couldn't believe my luck, as Wayne Gretzky was arguably the best player ever.

The next week at school, we showed our cards to our classmates and sorted them out at recess. One of my friends invited me over to his house to show his older brothers, who were hockey card collectors and figured they could tell me how much the cards were all worth. Feeling pretty cool to be in the presence of the older, even cooler high school boys, I showed up with my winnings.

After looking at my card, they told me, "Braden, these are good, but the Wayne Gretzky card is a fake and not worth anything. Sorry."

Seeing the disappointment on my face, they offered me a Montreal Canadiens poster and a few Montreal players' cards from the current year in exchange for the Wayne Gretzky card. Grateful for this small favor, I accepted and shook on it.

I went home but didn't tell my parents the bad news: that the Wayne Gretzky rookie card they thought was worth something was really a fake. A few months later, this friend of mine and his generous brothers moved to Calgary. After he left, some older boys in the school told me how the brothers had bragged about ripping me off by trading Wayne Gretzky's rookie card for a worthless Montreal Canadiens poster.

That day, I rode my bike home faster than I ever had before. I stormed into my room, ripped up the cards they gave me, sank down by my bed, and cried. It was my first real experience in broken trust, and I never forgot what that felt like. Not long after the trade, this family moved across the country. My card was gone, and I didn't tell my parents for months afterward.

But here's the kicker. It's not that I vowed never to do that to others. I was mad at myself for falling for their trickery. I believed it was my fault, that I should have known better, and good on them for getting the better deal at my expense.

But this led to some negative outcomes.

For a long time afterward, I would trick kids out of their sports cards or lunch snacks or anything else that I wanted. I was wounded, and I vowed to never be a victim again. It took a long time and a strong Spiritual Life to get me off this track.

How many leaders are operating with a wounded or warped worldview? How will that determine the type of impact they will have? Is there any belief that is causing you to think or act in a way that doesn't foster a positive outcome for everyone?

In the Foundations course at LeaderImpact, which every leader needs to do upon becoming a member, we engage in a Life History exercise. This exercise involves writing out life experiences, relationships, defining moments, wounds, and Spiritual Life in different stages, such as childhood, teen years, young adulthood, and the present. It doesn't take as much time as you think. If you've never done this exercise, it's extremely enlightening and shows you patterns in your life as a leader. Patterns such as mistrust, broken relationships, perseverance, or the support you received at critical moments. The accomplishments are typically the great memories, but the wounds (like my Wayne Gretzky rookie card moment) leave scars that can shape our behavior. Your Internal Self is the carrier of these high and low moments in your life. It's important to recognize and bring clarity to them so that your leadership is not inadvertently hindered or hijacked.

YOUR INTERNAL SELF

When your Personal Life engages with your Spiritual Life, this creates your Internal Self. Your Internal Self is where your thoughts, emotions, and behavior arise from. This is also known as character or identity. One my favorite definitions on character is that it's "who you are when no one is around." Your personal identity shaped by your beliefs and core values is your Internal Self.

Every action starts in the mind. If you don't control your mind, you cannot control your actions.

A leader who wants to have impact on others must be able to master their Internal Self. In James Allen's book *As a Man Thinketh*,[17] he goes deeper into the notion that thoughts ultimately produce circumstances.

> A particular train of thought persisted in, be it good or bad, cannot fail to produce its results on the character and circumstances. A man cannot directly choose his circumstances, but he can choose his thoughts, and so indirectly, yet surely, shape his circumstances.

The main battle in becoming a leader of impact is in your mind. There will always be tension between doing what you want versus sacrificing for doing what's right. These are your thought patterns that will determine your actions, which ultimately shape your circumstances.

For example, if you want to impact an employee but are always thinking how immature or naive they are, you can't behave in a way that will influence them positively. It won't work. There is no magic flip of the switch. Or if you try to master a new skill but keep saying to yourself that you can't or you're not good enough when you practice, you'll never end up mastering it. You have to start with your thoughts.

I attended the Hugh O'Brien Leadership Camp for tenth-grade students. One of the speakers handed out these neon yellow business cards with the big black letters "CYT" written across them. The letters stood for "Check Your Thoughts." He was encouraging us to continually check our thoughts to ensure they were positive, pure, and providing momentum.

Stop negative and impure thoughts early. You have the ability to control your thought life. Every action stems from a thought, so ensure you're thinking about the right things.

Your mind is a garden.
Your thoughts are the seeds.
You can either grow flowers.
Or you can grow weeds.

—ANONYMOUS

FAILURE IN THE HOME

As you move from your inner thoughts, your home life is the next area that truly reflects the strength of a leader's Internal Self. I serve on the board for the charity of my friend Stu McLaren, Village Impact. (Yes, I realize I'm becoming the impact guy in a lot of things I'm involved with.) One of the board members, David Frey, has a large poster in his home office that reads, "No amount of success can compensate for failure in the home." Every time we have a video conference call, I see this poster behind him, and it's such a great reminder. In the LeaderImpact global survey, 80 percent of the respondents who were married or in a committed relationship indicated they give a high amount of attention and importance to their spouse/partner. This is great to see, as this relationship is one of the most significant ones you will have.

Nothing ruins important relationships or reputation more than moral failure. I've had a chance to see this play out firsthand with a friend of mine, and it's ugly.

I'm one of four partners in a successful snack food company. In the seven years that we've owned this company, revenue has grown over 900 percent, and we're selling snacks across North America and, more recently, into Asia. One of the four partners is a friend of mine, and he's the one who introduced me to the opportunity. My friend is a prototypical entrepreneur. He has an endearing personality, has high energy, loves to solve problems, sees opportunity, and works like crazy to find solutions. He owns several businesses. He's been married for over twenty years, has four kids, and always appeared to have a strong Spiritual Life. He is generous with money, often mentored young leaders, and has compassion for others in need. He had mastered managing his External Life. To people on the outside, including me, he's a good leader.

But he screwed up. He had an affair—not just a one-time fling but an ongoing lie lasting for years. He knew his actions were wrong, but he didn't stop it.

Moral failure reaps carnage on a life. His marriage of over twenty years is forever changed and, without God's help, may not make it. His relationship with his kids is very different. He's hurt the business he is involved with, discouraged many people, broken relationships, and now has to repair his reputation, which will take time.

His ability to influence and therefore have impact has taken a major step back. But it didn't need to be this way. How did this happen to a good leader who knew better?

I was at a leadership conference with author John Maxwell. One of the surprising pieces of advice he gave was on marital faithfulness and moral character. He said, "Never think [an affair] can't happen to you." No one is above making a mistake. It starts in your mind with a thought. Then a small action. Then another thought and another small action. If your thoughts are not held in check and your actions are not held accountable, it will lead to a much larger and graver ending.

Regardless of the mess, there is hope. My friend recognizes the truth of his actions, and he takes responsibility. All he can do now is accept the consequences, start over, and get back on the right path. That's the good part of forgiveness. We can always get back into the game, regardless of how badly we've messed up. If you know someone who has been in this situation, I urge you to reach out and offer grace.

It's in these moments that people need others who will walk with them and help them get back on the right path. I know my friend is going to use this experience to help other leaders become better and to avoid the mistakes he made.

BEWARE OF YOUR LAST EMOTIONS

Your Internal Self is in a battle of the mind and of the will. As a leader who wants to have impact, it's important to say the right things, do the right things, and be the kind of leader worth following.

Have you ever snapped at your spouse or partner in a response that you know you shouldn't have? Have you lost patience with your kids or employees or that supplier? Have you done something that you've regretted? Yes. We all have.

In many cases, you momentarily lost your ability to master your emotions and reacted in the moment. There are four emotional states that affect your Internal Self. If you become aware of them, you can help mitigate these issues.

I call them your "LAST emotions." They're usually the last emotions you have before you do something that you'll regret. LAST is an acronym that stands for:

· Loneliness
· Anger
· Stress
· Tiredness

Think about a time when you did something that was inconsistent with who you are and who you want to be. In many of those cases, one or more of these emotional states was probably present.

LONELINESS

Isolation is dangerous, and unfortunately, it's common for leaders and busy executives to experience. A heavy travel schedule takes you away from consistent contact and relationships that keep you grounded and accountable. Many leaders find it difficult having close friends because of their position of influence. There always seems to be someone who wants something from you. In our survey, over 16 percent of respondents said they didn't have close friendships, and 47 percent said they have only one or two.

Relationships require communication, reciprocal actions, and shared experiences to strengthen—all of which take an investment of time that leaders don't have a lot of. Or at least choose not to have a lot of. This affects friendships, as well as your relationship with your spouse.

Loneliness can occurs in marital relationships. You're busy, you see and communicate with each other less, and you're not having regular sex. The result is loneliness, which can lead you to sexually related behaviors such as sexual thoughts toward others, pornography, strip clubs, or inappropriate sexual contact or flirting toward others. If these actions are not held in check and dealt with, it leads to affairs, "happy ending" massage parlors (like New England Patriots owner Robert Kraft), or worse, prostitution.

ANGER

Anger is typically experienced because of fear or sadness. Fear is about anxiety or worry. Sadness is about loss, disappointment, or discouragement. As a leader, you're paid to get results, and bad things happen when you don't achieve them. If you continue to miss targets and profitability, the company has to lay off employees, which affects not only the employee but their family and community too. You could lose investors and bankrupt the company. What happens if you lose your edge, and competition steals market share? What if you lose your biggest customers or if a major issue happens in your supply chain?

The amount of pressure mixed with fear creates a recipe for anger to occur. This is why peace and patience are such key traits from your Spiritual Life. If anger is allowed to take over, you will inevitably say or do something that will be damaging. It takes a long time to build trust and seconds to lose it.

STRESS

Stress can be experienced through higher amounts of emotional tension or mental strain. Welcome to leadership. Whether you like it or not, leadership brings mental strain because there's always tension in solving problems, making decisions, and being responsible for the consequences of those decisions on people and results. The key is how stress affects you personally.

Thirty-eight percent of the leaders surveyed allow stress to affect their well-being or are thrown off by stress in their life. Stress also weakens immune function and increases chances of heart disease.

Stress is part of a leader's life, but intense stress over a long period of time is a killer. Understand the root cause of the stress and look for ways to reduce it immediately. If it's time pressure, then move timelines, reschedule meetings, or set new expectations with stakeholders. Exercise. If it's money pressure, find new sources of investment, eliminate fringe expenses early, or create plans to generate new revenue streams. If it's people-related stress, talk to a counselor, bring in a consultant, confide in other leaders to help you see the situation differently. The right solution is only for you to decide, but realizing that you need a plan and solution is critical. Do not be content to just ride it out or weather the storm. Stress needs a release, or it causes damage, and you can't be a leader who has an impact if you're operating in stress mode.

TIREDNESS

Due to the nature of leaders' lives, mental and physical fatigue is fairly common. Consistent late nights finishing work. Poor sleep while traveling and moving between time zones. The constant mental strain of solving problems, coaching team members, working with customers or suppliers on a daily basis. Leaders have more energy than the average person, but every leader has limits. When you're tired, you don't have the energy for the best self-control.

This is the reason that rest (and sleep) is a crucial part of your Personal Life that we discussed. You need to plan time for rest, vacations, weekends, and taking off a Sabbath day. The Sabbath is separating one day out of the week where you don't work—at all. You rest, recharge, and reflect on your life, God, and relationships. Keeping the Sabbath day holy is so important that it was one of the ten commandments in the Bible. It joins the list of murder, adultery, stealing, and lying. It's that important, and yet many leaders still don't practice it. Do you trust God that if you take one day off, He'll help you be productive and successful with the other six days?

DEALING WITH LAST EMOTIONS

So how do you deal with these emotions? Think through them in a Personal, Professional, and Spiritual manner.

- **Personal: Be aware of them.** You have to recognize that what you are feeling is a symptom of one of these emotional states. It's affecting you and your judgment, so have self-control and don't make key decisions or say something that you'll regret.
- **Spiritual: Take time and pray.** Remove yourself from the situation if possible. Close your eyes and pray. Ask God to give you wisdom to know what to do, protection from doing anything stupid, and the strength to follow through with a plan. I remember driving back home from a tough day at work. I was tired, stressed, and angry. I knew if I walked into the house, my kids would want to jump all over me, and Jen would want to talk. I didn't have the strength, so I stopped the car a few blocks from the house. I closed my eyes and prayed. It was maybe ten minutes, then I continued home with a new focus, and the night went well.
- **Professional: Create a plan.** You can't stay in these emotional states. You're a leader, and you make plans and develop strategy all the time. Create an alleviation plan. If you're tired, schedule time in your calendar for rest. If you're stressed, understand the root cause and create a plan to alleviate the cause. If you're angry, understand where the anger is coming from and create a plan to address it. If you're traveling and lonely or lonely in general, schedule time to be social, or call a friend or family member. No one plans to fail; they just fail to plan.

KEYS TO REMEMBER

Your Internal Self is the identity you've created from your Personal and Spiritual Life. It starts in your thoughts, which are shaped from your values and drive your behavior. This is where becoming a leader of impact begins. To strengthen your Internal Self:

- **Understand your wounds.** Reflect on your life and the circumstances (good or bad) that have had an influence on your identity. These experiences determine how you see the world and can hijack your mind and behavior if they aren't dealt with.
- **CYT (Check Your Thoughts).** Continue to evaluate the thoughts you have to ensure they are positive, pure, and providing momentum for who you want to be. Stop negative and impure thoughts early. You have the ability to control your thought life.
- **Focus on your home.** Most leaders focus on their occupation first and ensure it's in order before fixing their home life. I want to challenge you to do the opposite. Focus first on your relationship with your spouse/partner and kids, if you have them. A peaceful and complete home provides the mental freedom and confidence to focus and be more present in your work.
- **Beware of your LAST emotions.** Loneliness, Anger, Stress, and Tiredness will be part of your life as a leader. Deal with it. Literally. Have enough self-mastery to recognize them, take a moment to slow down and pray, and create a plan to alleviate them.

Recently, a 1979 O-Pee-Chee Wayne Gretzky rookie card sold at auction for a record US$465,000. Sometimes, the best lessons are priceless. In this case, it came with a price, and yes, it still stings.

> CHAPTER 10 ⟨

GIVING OF YOURSELF (PROFESSIONAL AND SPIRITUAL LIFE)

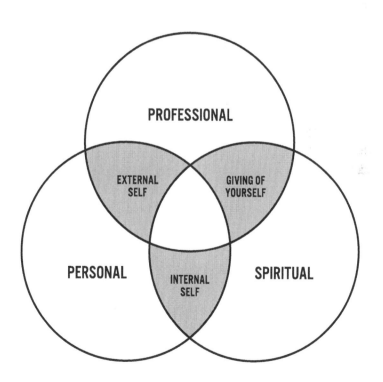

Giving of yourself is when your Spiritual Life and Professional Life integrate. It occurs when your career and beliefs align, and you begin to see positive results in people's lives. This is your contribution to impact on a tangible level. Chapters 4 through 9 were helping you to focus on *who* you are as the first and most important attribute to becoming a leader of impact, and now this chapter moves to *what* you can do as that leader.

You don't need to quit your job or change careers or join a nonprofit organization to be effective in impact. I actually tried that.

After my wake-up call, which I talked about in the introduction to this book, I knew I needed a change from marketing chips and climbing the corporate ladder at Frito-Lay. I went down the path of developing my Spiritual Life while working at Frito-Lay. My mind, soul, and life were changing, but I kept feeling this conviction to use my marketing skills to help others at a deeper level.

That's when I met Leonard Buhler.

"Braden, how would like to do work that makes a difference? I'd like you to lead our marketing and communications division at Campus Crusade for Christ," he asked.

I had never even heard of Campus Crusade for Christ before I met him, but he piqued my interest with doing work that made a difference. Leonard was a successful potato farmer who left his family business to become the president of this organization in 2004. He's a great salesman. He's full of passion, vision, and has a can-do approach that many entrepreneurs possess, which makes it easy to say yes to him.

"OK," I said. "I'll do it."

My Frito-Lay colleagues didn't understand the decision and felt it was a career-limiting move. My parents and family were supportive but didn't love the idea that I would be moving across the country to the West Coast. When I think back to this decision, it was a bit insane, but I was determined to make a difference.

However, after a short time of working at Campus Crusade, I realized something profound. Almost every strategy, project, and initiative at the organization needed business leaders to get behind them, help fund them, or push them along. These leaders, entrepreneurs, and executives had the affluence, influence, and skills that we needed. And without them, these projects or staff or ideas would never exist. There would have been no impact without their contribution.

I experienced firsthand how leaders can use their talents and resources to make an impact.

This is when I decided to start an agency to help businesses and leaders be profitable and enable them to use those profits for good. Working at the nonprofit wasn't a wrong choice for me. It was a great move to help me mature and get to where I am today, but nonprofits are not the only places that make a difference. Anyone, anywhere, in any job can be a leader of impact.

There is absolutely no doubt in my mind that if leaders gave of themselves more, they could impact people and the world in ways they could never imagine. You have more potential than you realize.

It's when your Spiritual Life integrates with your Professional Life that you start to see clearly how your skills can enable you to live a life of impact. Marketing chips wasn't a bad thing. Being a great investment banker is not wrong. Owning a paper company is not less meaningful than being a pastor at a church or saving the whales with Greenpeace. What matters is *who* you are and *what* you do with what you've been given.

If you have skills in paper selling, go crush that.

If you're an amazing designer, be the best in your field.

If you understand financial analysis, get after it.

Be a leader who sets the bar high, who cares for people, and then use the money you earn and the time you have to build into your relationships and support the causes you're passionate about. Make giving a part of your business and a part of your life. Don't hold back. Don't just save up a massive nest egg or always look for a lifestyle trade-up. Give of yourself.

You will inspire others to do the same. And that's how change in the world is made.

PEOPLE WANT COMPANIES AND LEADERS TO MAKE AN IMPACT

When you start to give of yourself, it's not just the people who experience the positive change that notice. Others notice too, and they're starting to want to see this and expect it. They expect to see impact from the companies they work for and want to know they are making a difference, regardless of the industry they're in.

According to a 2016 Cone Communications Study, three-quarters of millennials would take a pay cut to work for a socially responsible company. Eighty-eight percent of millennial employees say their job is more fulfilling when their employers provide opportunities to make a positive impact.[18]

In 2015 *Harvard Business Review* published an article entitled "The Truth about CSR."[19] The authors confirmed in their research that by participating in CSR (Corporate Social Responsibility) programs, the organization saw improved business performance, mitigated risk, and enhanced their reputation. These benefits were on top of the main benefit of being able to contribute to the well-being of the communities and society that they affect or belong to.

This notion of creating a better world through work is not isolated to leaders and employees. Consumers want and are demanding this from the products and services they buy. Nielsen reported that 66 percent of consumers (and 70 percent of millennials) are willing to pay extra for products and services that come from companies committed to positive social and environmental impact.[20] And according to another Cone Communications study, 94 percent of consumers are likely to switch brands (of about equal in price and quality) to one that supports a social issue.[21]

During the COVID-19 pandemic, it was amazing to see how many businesses and brands were giving and trying to make impact.

- Airbnb reduced rates and worked with hosts to provide 100,000 healthcare providers with a place to stay near their hospitals.

- TULA Skincare had an offer where if you buy one of their skincare masks, all proceeds would go to purchase face masks for the New York City healthcare providers.
- Danone donated $200,000 to the Breakfast Club of Canada organization to help feed the kids who used to rely on getting meals at school; belairdirect also donated $500,000 to that same program.
- Bauer, which makes hockey equipment, retooled its manufacturing to make face shields to supply the healthcare system.
- Zoom, the online video conferencing service, offered their service for free to schools and also dropped the forty-minute meeting time limit.
- Audible launched hundreds of free titles for children and students.
- Crocs donated 10,000 pairs of shoes every day to healthcare providers. At one point, they had 400,000 people waiting to receive them.
- Serta Simmons Bedding donated over 10,000 mattresses to New York City hospitals, and they were asking and inspiring other partners to do the same.
- Verizon donated $2.5 million to help local nonprofit initiatives during COVID.
- Even small local businesses like the Carvery Sandwich Shop in White Rock, British Columbia, delivered free meals to healthcare providers and hospitals each day, and they were ringleaders in challenging other restaurants to do the same.

And this is just a short list. There were hundreds and thousands of companies pitching in and donating millions of dollars. The cynical marketer in me knows that some of these businesses were trying to integrate cause marketing just to drive revenue and positive PR mentions. But many of them sacrificed and gave without any expectation of a return.

When you do the right thing without expecting anything in return, that's giving of yourself. That's what leaders of impact do.

If you're inspired to make giving a key part of your life and/or business, there are four things I recommend you keep in mind:

- **Stay in your lane.** Stay true to your purpose. When you're asking yourself or your team what you should be doing, and how, staying in your lane is key. For example, Zoom isn't going out and trying to do something that they don't excel in. They're giving away or providing their services to those who need it. Don't try to create a whole new division or element to your business. It's more important to look at your core competency and purpose and find ways to leverage and channel that.
- **Understand the need.** By this far into the book, you know that I put a lot of focus on people, and understanding what people need is a critical step in determining your actions. Instead of replicating what others are doing to give, ask nonprofits, government officials, customers, organizations in your area, or your employees first, "What do you need, and where can we help?" Reach out to your customers and ask them what issues they are dealing with that you could help with. Really understand the need before you jump in and start to do something.
- **Start small.** I can't emphasize this enough. When we hear the examples from COVID, it feels so big. You may feel inadequate because these other huge companies have the means and resources that you don't. The key is to start

small. Use what you have, where you have it, and just take that next step. Don't become paralyzed. Some leaders are prone to paralysis because they tend to think you have to do something big or cool or great. I don't think that's true. If you have a cause that you feel passionate about that aligns with the benefit of your product and service, just start to take small steps within that.

- **Be consistent.** You have to quell your expectations that it's going to lead to some massive return or great PR or that it will be easy. It's going to be more work and cost you a bit more than you thought. Prepare for that and be consistent in your actions. Whenever you do something for the first time, it's going to be scary. It's not going to feel good. You might ask yourself, "Am I doing this right? Is it even helping? Should we be doing this?" You're going to question a lot. My advice is to stay consistent, start small, and over time, you'll see the impact.

START WITH YOUR PERSONAL MISSION

It's easier to give, and you are more focused, when you have a personal mission that helps guide you. Many organizations have mission statements.

Jim Collins and Jerry Porras helped make mission, vision, and values famous in their book *Built to Last: Successful Habits of Visionary Companies*. The mission or purpose of an organization is the reason the organization exists. It serves as a guide for all actions and decisions to ensure alignment with their core behaviors, values, and identity in the market.

Starbucks has been a leader in coffee but also in pioneering programs, such as offering employee benefits and stock options to minimum-wage staff, which was revolutionary in the 1980s and 90s. They recently changed their mission statement: "To inspire and nurture the human spirit—one person, one cup and one neighborhood at a time."

Why would they do this? I believe the leadership at Starbucks knows it's important to make an impact not only for consumers and employees but also for investors and communities that they're a part of. Inspiring and nurturing the human spirit is far more invigorating to strategies, innovation, and performance than a mission that says, "We're going to make the best coffee in cool spaces."

A good mission captures emotion. The same is needed for you personally.

Forty-four percent of leaders surveyed in our LeaderImpact Assessment had a deep sense of purpose in all aspects of their lives. Another 43 percent felt purpose in certain areas, but surprisingly, only 21 percent felt only occasional or no purpose in their lives.

Your personal mission will help keep you focused on impact. What is your personal mission or purpose?

Many leaders find it easier to create a mission or purpose statement for their companies than for themselves. There's a lot of pressure to create the "right" one. We go through this exercise of creating one at LeaderImpact during Foundations. It's tough work and takes time. However, it's amazing to see the inspiration and clarity that it has on someone's life when they nail it.

It took me a while to refine my mission, but I finally found one that's stuck, and I've mentioned it throughout the book, if you caught it.

My mission is to help leaders find true success.

The people I feel drawn to help are leaders.

True success can be on a practical level where I'm literally helping leaders achieve financial gain or growth for their business. True success also means helping them in their Personal and Spiritual Lives with the conversations we're having and intention I have toward them as people. I also consider my wife and kids to be leaders, and I invest in them in that way. I have a large whiteboard in my home office, and this mission is written across the top in large block letters. It keeps me focused and reminds me of why I'm alive and what's important.

Here are a few pieces of advice as you develop your mission statement.

1. Don't try to find the silver bullet or wordsmith it to death. It can change over time.
2. Make sure it reflects you and your heart. This is not about propping yourself up and having a mission that others will admire. Your mission needs to guide and inspire you to be a leader of impact.
3. Own it. If you ask people for feedback on it, listen to them for improvements that make sense, but don't worry if it doesn't resonate with them. Your mission is not for them. It's for you. They can have their own, but you need to own yours.

Once you find a purpose, integrating elements of yourself to give becomes the next opportunity to ensure a contribution. This contribution could be supporting organizations or causes with your time and money. It could be leveraging cause marketing strategies like "buy one, get one free." Allowing employees to be engaged in the causes with you is also a great idea. For example, the organization Food for the Hungry has an impact business program that helps companies bring employees to developing countries, partner with a village, and then engage their network and customers at home to support change.

THE GOLDEN PLUNGER

Integrating your purpose can also mean instituting core values into your company that reinforce the purpose with employees too. This is something I've tried to do at my own company.

As you know, my business is marketing, which is classified as a professional service. Like other service businesses, we serve our clients to help them achieve a desired outcome. If you've ever worked in a service business, you'll know that it's not easy. You're constantly balancing the demands of your clients with the needs of the organization. In most cases, you don't have a choice of your clients either. Some can be dream clients, and others are brutal to work with, but I want to impact them all through how we serve them.

Knowing this is my desire, I wanted to hire people who really have a heart to serve. They obviously need to be smart and qualified for the role, but deeper than that, I want people who have humility, are not entitled, and are willing to go beyond their job description if we need them to. This is character and is the first core value at our company and is one of the core traits that leaders of impact possess.

This idea never became clearer to me than when we had an issue with one of our bathrooms at the office and an important meeting with a large client.

"Braden, the women's restroom is plugged and overflowing," our receptionist said.

It was 9:30 a.m. Our largest client was coming to our small, funky office for a brand presentation in thirty minutes. They had a number of females on their team, and I knew they would need to use the restroom. Our office had two small rooms for a male and female restroom. I'm a big believer that restrooms are a reflection of the level of service and care for people that an organization has. If they're cool and well cared for, the organization is one that thinks carefully about people and detail.

I walked into the restroom. Sure enough, the toilet was plugged and about to overflow. I went to the broom closet and retrieved the plunger. I tiptoed toward the toilet, not wanting to get any excess water on my dress shoes or suit. I cautiously dipped the plunger into the toilet and started to plunge it. Nothing happened. It wasn't working.

Just then, Hakon Fauske, my director of operations, came around the corner. He was a six-foot-four-inch Norwegian with a slight accent and positive personality.

"Braden, what are you doing?" he said.

"The toilet is plugged, and we have a presentation today in twenty minutes," I responded.

"You're doing it wrong. Give it to me. You need to get ready for the presentation," he said as he grabbed the plunger from my hand. He started to plunge it with vigor, and water was splashing everywhere. It was disgusting. I quickly slipped out of the small restroom and continued to prepare for the meeting.

With five minutes to spare, Hakon was able to fix the toilet, clean the floors and restroom, and have it looking like new in time for the clients to arrive. I was impressed. For one, he's an excellent plunger. More importantly, he didn't have to do it. He chose to. He was the director of the company, but he became a toilet cleaner for the sake of service. That was exactly the type of character I wanted for everyone at CREW.

That night, I bought a new plunger, and we painted it gold. At the next all-team meeting, I presented Hakon with the first Golden Plunger Award for going beyond his job description to serve.

He wrote his name on it with a Sharpie marker, and at the next all-team meeting, he presented it to someone else who showed that same trait of service above self. The Golden Plunger is now the highlight of our monthly team meetings. Over the years, it's been accepted and presented to dozens of employees, and each CREW office gives out their own. We've even created a Silver Scrubber Award, which is a dish scrubber with a silver ribbon on it that's presented to the runner-up for the month.

The language around this concept has even gone beyond team meetings to our hiring practices. The one question we ask each other after interviews with potential employees is: "Will this person be a plunger?" If we don't think so, we don't hire them. Period. We can't train character. It has to be who they are.

A strong spiritual life gives you the tools and beliefs for strong character that, when combined with your professional occupation, make way for giving of yourself. This is how leaders start to win and do work that matters.

WINNING AND METRICS IN IMPACT

Leaders of impact change how they define success and winning.

I come from a competitive family. This means we really like games, and we all really love to win. Every three years, there's a huge one-week family reunion with more than eighty people in attendance (my mom comes from a family of ten kids). It's a shock for anyone marrying into our family. They feel totally overwhelmed, but I think it's great. Most of our family trips growing up revolved around this reunion, and we've been able to see most of Canada because of them. Every day of the reunion has a theme like mini Olympics with camp games, golf tournament, sports days, and card tournaments. There's nothing more entertaining than watching your eighty-year-old uncle take out your seven-year-old cousin in the egg-on-a-spoon race.

This means the love of competition and winning is engrained. Almost all the leaders and entrepreneurs I know also love to win. They're competitive by nature, which gives them the drive to take risks, work hard, and accomplish more than most people.

But how you define winning and how you measure success is paramount. The father of management, Peter Drucker, is famous for the saying "What gets measured, gets managed." He's absolutely right. When it comes to businesses and organizations, what is chosen as a key measure of success is what will direct the decisions, actions, and behaviors of the people.

If you measure revenue and profitability, your actions will involve driving sales and cutting costs. If you measure market share, your strategies will focus on beating the competition. If you measure customer satisfaction, your behavior will focus on fulfilling customer needs.

Now take this idea and move it into impact. How should you measure it? I believe leaders don't spend enough time defining metrics of success for their life. Instead, they end up using money or time as the default metric.

If you are giving of yourself, what is the outcome of that gift? Does that align with your mission or purpose?

Just like finding and crafting your mission is difficult, so is finding the right metrics to measure success with. I have the following two metrics:

1. **The number of leaders I'm helping.** This can be through speaking, LeaderImpact, blog subscriptions, book purchases, family, and so on. It's also the number of relationships I'm building into intentionally (remember chapter 6, "Personal Life").

2. **The amount of money I'm giving away.** I want to make a lot of money and invest it with charities and organizations that are working with leaders to make an impact and to help people in need. My wife and I had a goal early in our lives to live off 10 percent of our income and give away 90 percent. We're not close to this yet, but it's a BHAG (Big Hairy Audacious Goal).

These metrics are not an exact science, and sometimes tracking them is difficult, but the intention and pursuit of them is the important step. I've kept my own metrics to two, as I know I'll get sidetracked if I try to have more. Once your metrics are clear, your annual goal-setting and strategies become much easier to create and live by.

FROM ENTREPRENEURS TO A VILLAGE IMPACT

I love being around leaders who understand the right metrics for success and who give of themselves. My close friend, Stu McLaren, runs a successful company called Tribe that helps entrepreneurs and organizations build and manage membership-based business models. He's probably the best in the world at it and makes great money. He could spend his well-earned cash on vacations, properties, other business ventures or socking it away for an eventual retirement or inheritance for his kids. But he hasn't done that.

With his wife, Amy, they used their skills, time and money and started a charity called Village Impact. I talked about this charity briefly in chapter 9. Their charity builds schools in Kenyan villages to help educate and inspire the next generation of leaders. The focus and hope is to break the cycle of poverty within rural areas. His company Tribe also donates hundreds of thousands of dollars a year to pay for the administration and charity. It's costing him and his partners a lot. But that's what a leader of impact does. They sacrifice and understand the cost. Through Village Impact, they are influencing the ongoing positive behavior within these students and teachers. It's an ambitious plan that's working.

But here's the best part—they aren't doing it alone.

Stu and Amy encourage and bring other entrepreneurs, friends, family, and clients to join them in this. They're influencing and impacting others to catch a vision for how to use business to impact more. They've raised millions of dollars, have numerous schools, and impact lives with a "village" of people around them.

Each time I hang out with Stu, I always leave feeling I'm not doing enough in the world. It's not depressing; it's motivating. There's a desire in all of us to become leaders of impact. Don't become a leader who has a lot but only gives a little.

KEYS TO REMEMBER

Giving of yourself occurs when your Spiritual Life and Professional Life align. To help you focus on this area, remember:

- **All work matters.** It doesn't matter what your product or service is; all work can matter. It's the impact you have on the people and relationships that makes the difference. Treat everyone with dignity, respect, and with genuine care. Limit the negative impact on people and the environment, and constantly be looking to add more value to society.
- **Be inspired by your mission.** Defining and clarifying your personal mission statement is a great motivator. Take the time to craft it and make it visible in your office and at home. Heck, even make a T-shirt or mug with the mission on it. Do whatever helps to make your mission real for you.
- **Define winning in your life.** Clearly defining the metrics that help to fulfill your mission will help you immensely to make an impact.
- **Give your LIFE.** Leverage your LIFE (Labor, Influence, Finances, and Expertise) to the purpose and cause you are

drawn to. Your return on this investment will be far greater than what you can buy or experience alone. Organizations and nonprofits, like Village Impact, are in desperate need of leaders to be involved in a big way. You have the ability to do a lot, and I challenge you to be all in.

One of my all-time favorite business books is Jim Collins's *Good to Great*.[22] There's a passage he uses to conclude his book, and it reveals a truth that this chapter is getting at.

> In the end, it is impossible to have a great life unless it is a meaningful life. And it is very difficult to have a meaningful life without meaningful work. Perhaps, then, you might gain that rare tranquility that comes from knowing that you've had a hand in creating something of intrinsic excellence that makes a contribution. Indeed, you might even gain that deepest of all satisfactions: knowing that your short time here on earth has been well spent, and that it mattered.

Choosing to be a leader of impact matters. And you can do that whether you're selling potato chips or building wells in Africa. It can all be good work that impacts others on the journey by using the gifts, talents, and resources you have.

CHAPTER 11

IMPACT (PROFESSIONAL, PERSONAL AND SPIRITUAL LIFE)

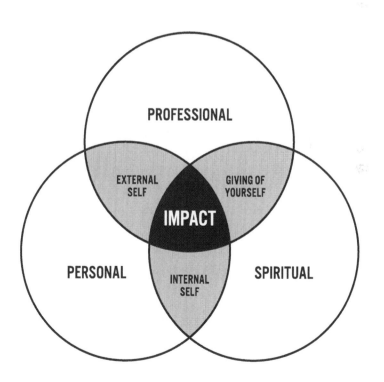

It's time to bring everything together. The convergence of professional excellence, personal optimization, and spiritual depth creates the right environment in a leader's life for impact to occur. Notice that I didn't say, impact will just automatically happen when these elements are together. There still needs to be a decision to be a leader who has an impact on others. There needs to be intention.

I wanted to find opportunities to make an impact when I was a young marketer at Frito-Lay. Every year, the Frito-Lay head office supported the United Way, which raises money for important community programs that serve the less fortunate in the city.

In this particular year, Frito-Lay employees created an auction with certain items that other employees could bid on to raise money. The auction had cool items, like NBA and NHL game tickets, autographed sports memorabilia, big-screen TVs, concert tickets, and so on. Employees also got creative and donated their executive parking spot for six months, a week of vacation, free lunch for a month, and other similar perks. But as I scanned the items, there was one item that really got my attention. You could bid on one hour with the president, Marc Guay. The description on the item said you could have him "clean your desk, write a report, review your budgets—whatever you wanted."

The bid on the paper started at seventy-five dollars. No one had their name on it yet. I quickly grabbed a pen and wrote my name down with the starting bid.

"Braden, what are you doing?" my colleague asked as she saw me write my name down.

"Seventy-five dollars is a good deal for an hour with the president," I said.

"You're new, so I'll let you in on something. Every year of the auction, only the VPs and executives bid on this one. I wouldn't do this if I were you," she informed me.

"Well, I'll probably get outbid anyway," I reassured her.

I didn't get outbid. I won an hour with the president for seventy-five dollars. Apparently, the whole company thought it was hilarious that this new kid in marketing was bold enough to bid on this item. They probably wanted to see the train wreck that would ensue and take side bets on how long I would keep my job afterward.

The next day, I went to the president's assistant to schedule in my hour.

"Marc has time to see you three months from now. Will that work?" she informed me.

"I'll take it." I said...as if I had a choice.

Three months was a long time to wait, but I guess a random hour with a young employee wasn't at the top of the president's priority list. It also bought me some time to think about what I was going to get him to do for me.

The time flew by, and there was only one week before my hour. I had a plan, but I didn't want to tell anyone.

"What are you going to get him to do?" my coworkers would ask.

"I can't tell you. It's a surprise," I would say.

The day before my hour with the president, the VP of Marketing, Dale Hooper, brought me into his office. He sat me down at a small table while he leaned against his large desk.

"So tell me, what are you going to have Marc do in your hour with him?" he asked.

"I can't tell you. It's a surprise," I said. I could tell immediately that he didn't like that response.

"Braden, I like you. I think you have a future here. You need to tell me," he said. His tone grew more stern.

"I'm sorry. I can't tell you. But you'll just have to trust me that it will be OK," I said.

"OK. It's your life," he said as he escorted me out of his office.

The next day came, and I was excited. I arrived at the president's office ten minutes before our scheduled hour and waited.

"Marc can see you now. He'll be a few minutes, but I'll show you in," his assistant said.

She escorted me into the large corner office. His desk was a deep-brown mahogany that sat adjacent to another sturdy round table with four chairs around it. The office was decorated with books, awards, and examples of some of the most famous snack food on it.

To my surprise, his assistant kept walking through the office and opened a side door. It led to a small executive conference room with a long table and eight chairs. There was a full bar and fridge filled with food, snacks, and different types of drinks. It was a whole new level. I got a glimpse of how the 1 percent had meetings. She sat me down at one end of the table.

"Hi, Braden, sorry to keep you waiting," Marc said. He had a slight French-Canadian accent and was tall with brushed-back brown hair.

"It's OK. Thanks for taking the time," I said. "I have something for our one hour together."

"Great. I'm curious to see what we'll be doing," he said.

I was nervous, my heart was pounding, but I was already committed, so I just went for it. I took out a sheet of paper with an Excel spreadsheet table. I had outlined a number of large projects I'd been working on for the past few months. Beside each project was a row of names of people who had been instrumental in that project, including suppliers, outside consultants, plant managers, finance personnel, and ad agencies. Beside each name was a specific element that they did well on for that project and their phone number.

"Marc, I'd like you to call these people and let them know on behalf of Frito-Lay that you appreciated their work on the project," I said.

"OK. It's your hour," he said.

I could tell he was a bit apprehensive of the prospect of calling these strangers, but he complied. There were about fifteen people he called, and 90 percent of the time, he left a voice-mail for them. This process took about forty minutes. We had twenty minutes left.

"Anything else?" he said.

"Just a few more things," I responded. I took out two cards from my portfolio.

"I'd like you to write these cards to the VP of Marketing and the director of Marketing to let them know what you appreciate about them and the work they've been doing," I said.

"OK," he said.

He took the cards and pen and started to write a small passage in each card. He placed them in the envelope when he was finished and wrote their first names on the front of each card.

This process took another fifteen minutes. I had five minutes left.

The last line on the Excel doc was the name of his wife and personal address and the number of a florist.

"For our last exercise, I'd like you to order flowers for your wife," I said.

"Really?" he said. "OK. It's your hour."

Marc dialed the florist number and ordered a bouquet for his wife. I had my credit card at the ready, but he waved his hand to gesture no, and he gave the florist his own Visa number.

"I'd also like to order another bouquet," he said.

He then put the phone receiver over his shoulder and asked me what my girlfriend's address was. That was a great surprise. I gave him the address, and he completed the order. Our time was now up.

"Thank you, Marc, for your time. I really appreciate it," I said.

"No, thank you. That was very different than what I was expecting, but in a good way," he said.

I left his office and delivered the two cards to my director and VP. They asked me how it went and what we did.

"Good," I replied. "We just talked about my projects and the people we work with."

The next day, I received a number of thank-you emails and voicemails from the people on the project list. One of the agencies actually forwarded the voicemail from Marc to their entire office as an encouragement. My girlfriend, Jen, who is now my wife, loved the flowers. More importantly, Marc came up to me a few days later.

"Thank you, Braden. It was a meaningful hour for me, and my wife loved the flowers," he said with a big grin and patted me on the back in a teammate kind of way.

My hope was to have an impact on him and the people I work with. I realized that it didn't need to be huge acts or take a lot of time or money to make a difference. It just took intention.

Intention is a plan. We never plan to fail; we usually just fail to plan. At this far into the book you should know *why* you want to become a leader of impact. You need to start with *who* you are going to focus on. Decide *what* you are going to do. Then place it in your calendar to ensure the *when* and *how* get done.

I'll use my wife Jen as an example that's close to home. She leads groups of women and teaches them to study the Bible. She's a great teacher and has hundreds of women join her online every Wednesday night. But I realized she needed a better setup at home. I placed it in my calendar to order lights, camera, a better microphone, and hired a contractor to build this out for us in our home office. God knows I'm useless with a hammer. It was going to take work and some money. But what does this show my wife? That I'm invested in her. I'm encouraging her in her gifts and sacrificing time and money to see her do well. Where is the impact? I'm helping her excel, and she's helping more people in turn.

This is a small example. But that's where impact starts.

Where can you be intentional with your influence and impact on others? How could you surprise, encourage, or support your spouse? Your kids? Your employees or your customers? Which nonprofit could you partner with?

Keep looking for opportunities, make a plan, and then execute right away. This is how leaders of impact start and keep going.

A LEADER OF IMPACT

How do you know what a leader of impact looks like? How do you know when you yourself or others are living this out? In my experience, there are seven main features that are evidence. These may vary in degree, but the principles of these features taken from the themes we've discussed hold true.

THE SEVEN MAIN FEATURES

1. Is driven by a **fulfilling purpose** that is focused on the betterment of others.
2. Confronts and **resolves conflict** in relationships with diligence and care.
3. Displays **gentleness and patience** in the midst of stress, tension, or frustration.
4. Is **generous** with their advice, time, and finances to people and causes they are drawn to and feel passionate about.
5. Is **disciplined** with their personal health, development goals, and activities to ensure they have the energy and capacity for the people and projects that matter.
6. Is in **community** with other like-minded people who hold them accountable, encourage them, and spur them on toward greater things.
7. Is **intentional** about having an impact on others.

When I look over this list and reflect on my own life, I realize there are times when I feel I'm hitting all the features and times when I feel like a total failure. If it's a pendulum, I'm swaying back and forth. I've come to realize over the years that this pendulum feeling is normal. Life happens and you have different seasons in your life. But overall, you should see progress as a leader as you're intentional and seize opportunities of impact.

A DYNAMITE LIFE

In 1864, a thirty-one-year-old Alfred Nobel was experimenting with explosives while working at his family's manufacturing facility in Sweden. A large explosive accident took the lives of five people, including Alfred's younger brother Emil. Alfred was devastated from the loss. Whether he blamed himself or not, we're not sure of, but it propelled him to search for a safer explosive. In 1867, Alfred patented a mixture of nitroglycerin and an absorbent substance, which he named "dynamite." Boom—fortune at his fingertips. But that wasn't the impact.

In 1888, Alfred's brother Ludvig died while in France. A French newspaper published Alfred's obituary by mistake instead of Ludvig's. Can you imagine someone sending you an obituary from France that was about your life and death? What would it say? Unfortunately for Alfred, the fake obituary was not kind to him. It condemned Alfred for creating dynamite and bringing so much death to the world from nations using it as a military explosive. He was shaken. He was fifty-five at the time, and this was not how he wanted to be remembered or the legacy he wanted to leave on this earth.

What could he do? What would you do if you were him?

Nobel was an inventor. Could he inspire other inventors to achieve, create, and invent for a greater good? Alfred set aside a bulk of his estate to establish the Nobel Prizes. These monetary and public awards would honor men and women for outstanding achievements in physics, chemistry, medicine, literature, and for working toward peace.

He didn't get to see a lot of prizes given away. A few years later, when Alfred was sixty-six, he died of a stroke in Italy. His estate left $250 million (today's USD equivalent) to fund the Nobel Prizes. He left a legacy that would impact millions.

Wouldn't it be nice to have a quarter billion dollars to leave an impact with?

But the amount is not what's important. It's the intention. Alfred had to create the idea, put it together, involve the right people, and ensure that it would continue after he died. He had to have a good plan. It wasn't left to chance. He had accumulated a lot, and subsequently, he gave a lot. He was being responsible with what was given to him. He shaped the change he wanted to see in the world.

FROM HOCKEY LEGEND TO LEADERSHIP LEGACY

Another leader who took what they were given and used it to make a lasting impact was Paul Henderson.

"Braden, God took a junk goal in the 1970s and used it in a powerful way," Paul said to me one day.

If you don't know who Paul Henderson is, he's a Canadian hockey icon. He was a professional hockey player in the National Hockey League in the 1960s and 70s. But his rise to fame happened when he competed for Canada in the 1972 Summit Series, which was an eight-game standoff against the Soviet Union. It was the first time professional hockey players were able to play in an international competition, and the world wanted to see the best two countries compete with their best players. Four games were played in Canada and four in the Soviet Union. Since it occurred during the Cold War era, the tensions were high.

Paul scored the game-winning goals in game six and again in game seven, but amazingly, his most famous goal would come in the eighth game with the score tied. Paul scored the game-winning goal again with only thirty-four seconds left. The whole of Canada went ballistic, and the image of Paul jumping and being mauled by his teammates would be seen for decades to come. It was hailed "the goal of the century."

But it was just a goal in a game where you skate on ice and put a rubber puck in a net. However, Paul's playing career and goal created a platform for him. Hockey gave him influence. What he did with that influence is what separates him as a leader of impact.

Paul had a great Professional Life in hockey. His Personal Life was solid as well. He married Eleanor, his high school sweetheart. They have a fantastic marriage with three children and now seven grandchildren. Paul and Eleanor were speakers with FamilyLife for years and helped other couples on how to have a strong marriage. Paul is also a motivational speaker and has spoken before thousands of people at some of the biggest corporations in Canada.

However, the thing that really separates Paul is his Spiritual Life. Paul became a Christian and gave his life to God when he was playing for the Toronto Toros in 1975. When the Toros moved to Birmingham to become the Birmingham Bulls in the late 1970s, Paul met John Bradford at his church, and it changed his life.

"Paul, why don't you join my men's discipleship group?" John asked him. "It's a bunch of other young guys that need to put down stronger roots in their Spiritual Life. I think you'll like it."

"Sure. I'll come," Paul said.

This group changed Paul's life. For three years, John taught the guys how to spend time with God, what it meant to live faithfully, and how to be leaders. When there was a need to start another group, John knew who to ask to lead it.

"Paul, there are some guys that have come to faith, and I need a leader to run this group," John said.

"OK. But I can't lead the group the way you do," Paul said.

"You shouldn't. Lead it in your own way and set the pace you want," John said.

Paul took up the challenge and led this group for a number of years. He loved it. He set a high standard for the group from the very beginning.

"We start on time and end on time. And if I come prepared, then I expect you will too," he would say.

In 1984, after retiring from professional hockey, Paul moved back to Canada. He leveraged his Canadian fame with Athletes in Action and spoke to schools, businesses, and sporting events for more than a year. Then in 1986, he wanted to get back to leading groups. There was nothing like the groups he experienced in Birmingham, and he wanted to get it going in Canada. He talked with three businessmen about his vision, and together, they started one group in downtown Toronto. Not long after, a lawyer named Fred Christmas asked if Paul could lead a group in his city of Hamilton. Paul jumped at it. Paul's vision was to have twenty-five groups of leaders that were seeing real-life change, and he called it the Leadership Group.

In 2007, the Leadership Group merged with Leadership Ministries to form LeaderImpact, which now operates in over twenty-five countries around the world, with hundreds of groups and thousands of leaders involved. His model of groups is still being used today.

Paul used his platform to have influence with leaders that changed their lives. His sacrifice and work created a movement worth following and a life of impact. You can do the same.

THE TROUBLE WITH OIL

I've used some big examples of leaders who had a large platform, but you don't need to be a celebrity or professional athlete to have an impact either. Bruce Edgelow is a business executive who finances and works heavily in the oil and gas industry. In 2015, the price of oil plummeted, and it continued with no answer in sight. As one of the largest lenders, his company was on the hook for millions of dollars. He had a plan for impact.

Bruce called a large meeting with the CEOs and presidents of companies that owed them money and were struggling. All the invitees came.

When everyone arrived, the room was thick with anxiety. Executives who were on top of the world a few years earlier were now facing the worst economic situation in their careers. A few experts opened the meeting by discussing the current and future state of the oil industry, and then Bruce got up to address the group. Many of the people in the room expected Bruce to lay into them for wasting money, bloating budgets, and poor planning, but he didn't.

He took this opportunity to address something deeper.

Bruce shared how he, as a leader, finds hope when circumstances are bad. He talked to them about stepping up as leaders in tough times, the importance of family and relationships, and he shared how his personal faith provides perspective on his identity.

Bruce basically taught them how to become leaders of impact in their Professional, Personal, and Spiritual Lives. It's beautiful. When you teach and move people toward ongoing positive behavior, that's impact.

The feedback from the attendees at the meeting was outstanding too. It was one of the best meetings Bruce has organized. He took a chance and leveraged his influence to have an impact on the lives of leaders who, in turn, will impact others they lead.

Do you see how any leader can live a life of impact? It can be an intentional gesture that impacts someone close to you. It can be a small action that grows into something larger. It can be a foundation that carries on a legacy.

Impact occurs when your Professional, Personal, and Spiritual Lives are optimized and aligned.

KEYS TO REMEMBER

I truly believe leaders have the potential to change the world. We need people like you to step up and lead a life of impact. To help you do this, remember:

- **Commit to impact.** Wanting a strong Professional, Personal, and Spiritual Life will take a commitment to do the work. You won't be perfect—no one is. But you will keep improving if you're willing to stay with it. This is not a diet to try and see if you get results. This is a life decision. A decision to say that you want to become a leader of impact.

- **Look for opportunities.** Every person or organization we engage with creates an opportunity for impact. Be open. Be available. Be intentional. Can you speak encouragement into someone's life? Can you send a rising star to a needed training opportunity? Can you help an employee's family member dealing with addiction? Can you surprise your spouse with a fun date night or a small gift? Can you support a charity with your business in a bigger way? Can you buy an hour with a president? Just saying.

- **Plan for impact.** When you see an opportunity, start to plan for impact. What are you going to do, how are you going to do it, and by when? I have found I need to schedule everything, even the spontaneous actions. This ensures it gets done. Remember that there is no impact without action.

One of Michael Jackson's hit songs from his album *Bad* was designed to bring some "sunshine into the world." This would have been especially important during the COVID-19 pandemic. The title was "Man in the Mirror." A portion of the proceeds from the song in the 1980s went to Ronald McDonald House for kids living with cancer. The premise of the song is simple. If you want this world to be better, you have to be the one to change first. You can even try a good MJ shriek as you sing along to it.

The king of pop was right. If you want to be a leader of impact, it starts with you. But you can't do it alone.

CHAPTER 12

NO ONE SUCCEEDS ALONE

I was watching an interview of a man who built a successful car dealership group in Michigan. He was touring his mansion, and he walked into his grand courtyard in the middle of his house. In the center was a round fountain and statue in the middle of it.

"This is my favorite piece of art in the entire house," he said gesturing to the monument-style statue. "It's the *Self-Made Man* by sculptor Bobbie Carlyle. And I just love it. It speaks to my life and success."

I sat there and just felt sorry for him. Sure, he was successful and had to overcome obstacles and a tough family upbringing, which is admirable. But he missed an important truth.

No one succeeds alone. Ever.

Whether or not they recognize it is the issue.

Imagine working for someone or with someone who really believed they were self-made. Would they be open to feedback and correction? Would they delegate effectively and give autonomy to others? Would they develop people around them and allow them to succeed or surpass them? Probably not. It would be stifling and most likely create a narcissistic culture.

You can have financial success but not make an impact. At least not in the way we define it.

There's a team we all need apart from the one at the direct business or organization. Don't get me wrong; the team in your work is key, and you need each other to achieve results, but for the purpose of impact in your life you need another team. These are people in your life who play a specific role that's needed to keep you on track.

I call it your GPB, and it stands for Guard, Pusher, and Board.

GUARD

Think of the Kevin Costner and Whitney Houston movie *The Bodyguard*—classic movie that definitely starts to show my age. Kevin Costner was a great bodyguard for a famous singer played by Whitney Houston. His job was not only to protect her from immediate danger but also to plan ahead and warn her about pitfalls, behavior, or actions that could lead to something harmful.

As a leader, you have influence and play an important role in life. If you want to have impact, you need to guard yourself from actions, behaviors, or circumstances that could harm you, discredit you, or take you off track. More often than not, you can't always see these things, which is why you need a guard.

Growing up, my mom was my guard, as I imagine many parents would be. My mom would watch out for me, keep me accountable for my actions, and even force me to rest when I needed it. I remember hating some of this at the time, but it's what I needed. Now, my wife, Jen, is my guard. She knows me better than I know myself. She'll let me know when I'm working too much or not getting enough sleep. She'll remind me to spend intentional time with her and the kids, as I have a tendency to get distracted and wrapped up with work. She'll let me know if I'm not thinking about a subject with the right perspective. It can be enormously frustrating at times, but I know I need it. And because she loves me, I know she's protecting me for my own good so that I can do the things that matter and be the leader of impact for the people who matter.

You need a guard in your life. A spouse, partner, family member, close friend, or someone who knows you well and loves you. They will keep you accountable and help you not only establish boundaries but stay within them. If you do have one, make sure they know you appreciate their protection. If you don't, start to find them or become a guard for someone else, and you'll see them do the same for you.

PUSHER

If you've traveled to Tokyo, Japan, and experienced the subway at rush hour, you'll have noticed the *oshiya*. These are train pushers. Dressed in their formal uniform, their role is to ensure all the passengers have boarded and no one is caught in the doors. They're more famously known for giving you a gentle but firm push into the train if needed. It's a great mental image for someone you need on your team—a pusher.

As the name implies, a pusher gets you moving in the right direction. They'll push you to go out of your comfort zone or help you take that next step you've been holding off on, and they'll ensure you're not getting stuck in life. They motivate you.

A friend of mine, Nathan Hildebrandt, is a pusher. He's on the global team at LeaderImpact and is known for giving leaders a push to start living a life of impact. He's not pushy, but he's also not shy in presenting an opportunity and giving you a push to take it. When I traveled to El Salvador with Leader-Impact in 2004, I was nervous. Nathan was leading the trip with about forty other leaders from North America, and we were speaking with business leaders and students at universities on values, business strategy, and the importance of your spiritual life.

"Braden, we'd like you to speak to a large group of young professionals tomorrow night," Nathan told me.

"I'm not really prepared. I don't think it's a good fit," I said.

"Nonsense. You'll be great. I'll tell them you said yes," he said in an enthusiastic tone that made it clear I didn't really have a choice.

I did end up speaking to the young professional group. I wasn't prepared and didn't feel like I could deliver anything great. My nerves were running high, but Nathan pushed me to do it.

And guess what? Many of the young professionals came up to us and said how much that impacted them. It ended up being the highlight of the trip for me and gave me a renewed vision and passion for helping leaders. Nathan's push was exactly what I needed.

We all need pushers in our life to help us take action. Listen to them. As Pablo Picasso, the famous artist, once said, "Action is the foundational key to all success." Sometimes you need a gentle but firm push to get you there.

BOARD

As a leader, you're required to make decisions all the time. It's why you get paid the big bucks. How to make the right decisions in different situations when there are a lot of right ways to go is the difficult part. It's the reason there are thousands of books on leadership to help us navigate and create strategies to do that.

But there is a solution in place for leaders that's tried and true. A board.

Do you know why public companies have a board of directors as part of their mandatory governance structure? To help leaders make better decisions. Companies know that a leader needs other opinions, skillsets, experiences, or connections to help them make the decisions that will lead to growth and to keep them accountable and on track.

As this chapter is trying to help you understand, you can't be as effective alone. You need a board. I work with entrepreneurs and one of the reasons they enjoy being an entrepreneur is the freedom they have. However, many groups and organizations such as YPO (Young President's Organization) or Vistage or EO (Entrepreneur Organization) or LeaderImpact have grown rapidly because they fulfill a need in a leader's life. Leaders need a safe place to talk about business and life issues, and to receive advice from objective people to help them navigate their world.

Whether you join a group or start your own advisory board, you need people who know you and who have the experience to give you the right advice.

King Solomon, who was regarded as one of the wisest kings in history, gave this proverb: "Plans go wrong for lack of advice; many advisers bring success."[23]

Have a board in your life, and you'll see that collective advice does bring better success.

MENTORSHIP

The topic of mentorship comes up often with leaders, especially with young and aspiring leaders.

Less than 10 percent of the leaders in our survey have a mentor who is committed to their development in all aspects of life. Another 32 percent have a mentor in their workplace whether it is a supervisor or direct report. Just be careful: there's always a caveat with work-related mentors in that the employment agreement typically gets in the way. Do they really care about you as a whole person, or are they more concerned with what the organization needs from the role you occupy and how to get you to be more productive? It's a fine line.

Knowing what you want from a mentor, why you want one, and finding one is very difficult.

When I worked at Frito-Lay, the HR department created a mentoring initiative that selected younger employees and teamed them up with a manager or director from another function. My mentor was an operations director who oversaw production in one of the chip plants. We would meet every two weeks for an hour or lunch and get to know each other, discuss what was happening, and answer questions I had about career development or the business.

He was a good guy, but the relationship, and eventually the program, fizzled out. These are the initiatives that start with such promise, die off, and then just get filed away into the corporate closet of failure. The intention of creating cross-functional relationships was great. Connecting young leaders with a seasoned vet is brilliant. Sustaining a relationship based on mutual trust is difficult. Would I be able to be totally open with him? To let him know I'm doubting my employment at Frito-Lay? To point out insecurities or vulnerable areas in my character? Heck no. The chances of him sharing that with my director or HR would be too much of a career risk.

After about the fourth time we met, we both ran out of the surface questions and business-related strategies to discuss. He also didn't really know how to progress a relationship or develop someone outside his functional area. I guess the HR mentor training had its limits. We both wanted it to work. But it didn't. Others in the program had a similar experience, which is why it fizzled, and we found other, more productive, areas to spend our time on.

Formal mentor relationships that work are very rare. If you've found one and it's working, cherish it. I think many leaders wish they had a business icon like Warren Buffett or Peter

Drucker as a mentor. They picture themselves meeting regularly together, laughing, strategizing, crying, and being motivated by them to achieve greatness. A celebrity mentor is not going happen for 99.8 percent of you. But it doesn't have to.

In speaking with many leaders, they are typically mentored by a number of people at various times in their lives. Seek out people in your life and be intentional to have coffee with them. Have questions prepared, and don't be afraid to ask the deeper ones. Mentors want to share knowledge, but many of them don't know where to start or what you need. You have to take charge of your life and ask what you need.

Just as you may want to have a mentor, there are leaders who want to be mentored by you. Take the time for them, but don't own the relationship: the mentee has to be hungry and desire your input. It's like the old saying, "When the student is ready, the teacher will appear."

THE YOKE FELLOWS

Remember Dr. Keith Dindi from Kenya, who I mentioned in chapter 6? He has a small group of four friends that are a great example of the importance of being with other leaders.

"We call ourselves the 'Yoke Fellows,'" he said. "It's an intentional group that ensures we live the life of impact we are meant to. We're not afraid to ask each other the tough questions, like marital relationships, business ethics, and spiritual life accountability. We pray and encourage one another. Without a doubt, we have each other's backs. I value this band of brothers, and we've worked hard over the years to maintain this relationship."

I loved hearing this from him. There are two important aspects of his Yoke Fellows that I feel are important to emphasize for you. First, they have each other's backs. They're not willing to let their friends make dumb mistakes and are willing to ask the tough questions, which could risk offending them. But this is what true friends do.

Secondly, they have worked hard to maintain this relationship. Building a friendship group in which you get to the point of naming it, like the Yoke Fellows, takes time. It takes effort to foster deep friendships, which is why, as a leader, you probably won't have too many of them. I haven't always been good at keeping in touch with people and fostering friendships. Sometimes it's been a season when life is busy with young kids and a growing business that I just couldn't find any spare time. However, I realize now, that's a poor excuse. Work hard to keep in touch and foster good friendships. It doesn't have to mean a lot of extra time. Just extra intention and maybe a golf weekend each year or so. The right friends are like gold. Their value always appreciates, especially when times are tough.

KEYS TO REMEMBER

No one succeeds alone. We all need people in our lives to help us grow professionally, personally, and spiritually. We also need to be the people that others need to help them grow. Here's some advice to help you become better together:

- **Thank your guard.** The guard is such an important position in your life. Usually we undervalue or take them for granted. Take some time this week to do something special for the guard in your life. Buy them dinner. Send them a gift. Let them know you appreciate them in your life.

- **Be pushy.** Just like I needed a push to step out and speak, someone needs that from you. Look for opportunities to push people in their areas of giftedness. Push someone to lead the meeting. Give a young leader a special assignment. Say yes to your kids in an area of new responsibility. They will not do it as well as you could, but the growth in their life will take a giant step forward.
- **Mentor someone.** You can't tell someone you'd like to mentor them. A mentee has to be the one to initiate and own the relationship. But often, young leaders don't know how to ask or what a relationship looks like, so you might need to prod them. Invite a young leader for coffee or a meeting and start by asking them questions in the three areas of impact: Professional, Personal, and Spiritual. Take an interest in young leaders and look for opportunities to share your wisdom and experience with them if they're open to it. If the young leaders are not hungry to learn, don't waste your time. Let ripe fruit rot. Focus on the green and growing ones.
- **Foster your own Yoke Fellows.** If you have friends in your life as close as the Yoke Fellows—cherish them. Keep asking each other the tough questions. Be committed to each other's impact in life. Do not let them go down the wrong paths or get caught up in the wrong activities. Be the friend that has their backs. Always.

Mother Teresa knew the value of teamwork and working together. A popular quote attributed to her serves as a great reminder.

I can do things you cannot.

You can do things I cannot.

Together we can do great things.

If you want to achieve great things, don't think like a self-made man. No one succeeds alone.

THE LAST CHAPTER

PREPARING FOR IMPACT

You now know that impact is not the same as helping. Impact is your actions that leave a perpetual positive behavior or change in someone's life. It occurs naturally when your Professional, Personal, and Spiritual Lives are optimized and aligned.

You now know how to be a leader who can impact:

- You are a great professional with increasing competence. Your three Ps are rocking—Passion, Pursuit of excellence, and Perseverance.
- Your Personal Life is intentional and under control. You understand that you can't lead others if you can't lead yourself. You're taking care of your mind and body to ensure you have high energy. You're intentional about the relationships and people in your life. Your marriage and family life is strong. You are disciplined with your time.
- Your Spiritual Life is alive and meaningful. You are on a journey to know God personally and to be changed from the inside out. You are moving from self-focused to other-

centered. Your thoughts, motives, and desires are centered on truth, and you are loving others genuinely.

- You are moving toward and ready for impact. You see your work as an intentional gift that you get to give every day. People in your life recognize a change and are thanking you for the difference you're making in their lives. You are starting to recognize opportunities to impact others and are using your talent, time, skills, money, and influence to help others.
- You're not trying to be a hero and are motivated for impact out of the glory or prosperity it may bring. You have found a cause and people you care about. You have a personal mission and purpose statement, and you sacrifice your time, attention, and money to fulfill that purpose.
- You're not alone. You have or are looking for your GPB (Guard, Pusher, and Board) to ensure you stay the course, are encouraged, make good decisions, and have fun along the way. You have people who know you, are like you, and who will not let you live a life of selfishness or mediocrity.

Growing up, my favorite TV show was the cartoon *G.I. Joe*. It's about the best US military soldiers fighting against the evil organization of Cobra. It was amazing military propaganda. Every episode would end with a life lesson for kids—for example, what to do if you get a cut and start bleeding. The G.I. Joe character would tell you how to apply pressure on the wound and go to an adult for help. But they always ended every lesson with the words "Now you know...and knowing is half the battle."

If half the battle is knowing, the other half is doing something about it. You know what impact is, but applying it and doing something about it is a whole new game.

Just start to play because you're the only player for your position.

YOU ARE BEING PREPARED

You have been groomed for a purpose. And you'll continue to be groomed. The experiences (good and bad) throughout your life have shaped you and provided you with resources to use for a bigger purpose.

Think about your career opportunities. The people who took a chance on you. The education, projects, and initiatives that have given you the skills and experience you have. The places you've visited. The family that you were born into. The friends that you've made. Your immediate family you have now. Your interests and passions.

There is no one like you. There will never be anyone like you again.

We are not meant to make the same impact as each other. We all have different roles to play and different ways to impact others. This is why we need each other if we're going to see positive changes in this world. The more leaders stepping up and impacting others, the more positive changes we'll see.

That's how a movement is made. Each person focuses on doing what they can and inspires others to do the same.

MOSES WAS PREPARED

Moses was probably the leader with the most impact in Israel's history. He led them out of Egypt after four hundred years of slavery; helped establish their laws, traditions, and governmental structure; and led them militarily against nations that wanted to wipe them out. Most people know the story or have seen the movies, like *The Ten Commandments*, *Exodus: Gods and Kings*, or *Prince of Egypt*, but what they don't usually know is how God prepared Moses—even when Moses was reluctant.

In conversations I have with people, I find they place a heavy emphasis on the spiritual development of leaders from the Bible. It's true there's a true love for God and commitment that's needed. But when God wants to use a leader for impact, he also prepares them professionally, personally, and spiritually. It's not random, and it's not only the person who has the spiritual depth who is chosen for important tasks.

Moses needed to accomplish one of the most important tasks in Israel's history. He needed to be groomed. There was no formal education for Israelites in his time. They were slaves. How would Moses, an Israelite, have learned about language, laws, government structure, and military tactics? God had to make a way for it.

When Moses was a baby, the Egyptian Pharaoh ordered all boys under the age of two to be killed, as he was afraid of an uprising one day. Moses's mother placed him in a basket along the Nile River to avoid the soldiers. The Pharaoh's daughter happened to find him and brought him back to the palace. She adopted him as her own, and Moses received the same privilege, education, and opportunity as a member of the royal household.

No one could have predicted this would be the way to educate an Israelite. But professional development is not enough to have impact, and Moses wasn't ready. Look at what Moses does, as told in Exodus 2:11–12 ("The Message").

> Time passed. Moses grew up. One day he went and saw his brothers, saw all that hard labor. Then he saw an Egyptian hit a Hebrew—one of his relatives! He looked this way and then that; when he realized there was no one in sight, he killed the Egyptian and buried him in the sand.

An educated and zealous leader was ready to lead. In his first encounter, he loses his temper, takes matters into his own hands, and kills a man. Not exactly the best start for a future leader. He's forced to flee the country and live in the wilderness of Midian.

Moses needed time to refine his personal and spiritual life. It took him forty years in Midian. That's a long time. I need that time frame to soak in so I'm not so impatient in my own life. Moses needed to get married, have kids, and learn the value of hard work and perseverance. He needed to live in the desert and understand how to live there, as Israel would end up wandering in that desert for forty years. Most importantly, he needed humility and a reverence for God. His spiritual life was being formed. We don't know what Moses did while he was a shepherd in Midian. I bet he prayed and talked to God, as there wasn't anyone else to talk to. I think he thought about God and would probably recite stories about him while walking.

But when Israel was ready and Moses was ready, God called him from a burning bush.

> "The Israelite cry for help has come to me, and I've seen for

myself how cruelly they're being treated by the Egyptians. It's time for you to go back: I'm sending you to Pharaoh to bring my people, the People of Israel, out of Egypt."

Moses answered God, "But why me? What makes you think that I could ever go to Pharaoh and lead the children of Israel out of Egypt?"

"I'll be with you," God said.[24]

Moses's response to God's call was humble and timid. There was also a mix of shame from what he had done when he was in Egypt. Moses wasn't motivated for the legacy he would leave in history. He didn't even want it even though he was ready. God had to pump him up, give him confidence, and show him through miracles that he would be with him, that it would turn out OK.

You can usually tell when you're ready to make an impact when there's a bit of reluctance even though you have the right skills and experience. There's a maturity in understanding what true impact costs.

It's been decades since my great wake-up call. I still feel I'm waking up and learning how to live a life of impact. It's not an event or skill to learn or something to add to your LinkedIn profile. It takes a lifetime to master through day-by-day actions, but the results will astound you.

If you're open to it, I encourage you to join a LeaderImpact group in your city or start one or find another group that helps you along this journey. Share this book with another leader and start to build into their life. I hope this impacts them as much as it has you. Let me know how you're doing in this journey of impact. You can contact me at BradenDouglas.com.

THE TIME THAT IS GIVEN YOU

J. R. R. Tolkien was the author of *The Lord of the Rings* trilogy. He lived in the early twentieth century, when the world was at war, and many of Tolkien's characters, battles, and narrative of the series were inspired by the world he was living in.

I recently rewatched *The Lord of the Rings* movies with my son, who's now old enough to really get the story and not be freaked out by the orcs. If you've never read the books or seen the movies, you should be publicly shamed. It's fantastic. The series should be required reading in school. Although my wife will attest that they're a guy thing.

Regardless, there's a beautiful exchange between Frodo—the Hobbit who has to carry the ring of power to Mount Doom in order to destroy it—and Gandalf, the wise wizard, who's not with Frodo anymore at this point. They've just lost a battle with the enemy. A good friend has been killed defending them, and the Orcs have carried away their other Hobbit companions. Frodo is discouraged and angry.

"I wish the ring had never come to me. I wish none of this had happened," Frodo says.

Frodo hears the voice of Gandalf: "So do all men who live to see such times, but that is not for them to decide. All you have to decide is what to do with the time that is given you."

Your position of influence and leadership is a gift that has been given to you. We can never choose the time that we are given or the circumstances.

Some moments will be peaceful. Others may be pandemics. Most will be in between.

My question to you is, what are you going to do with your leadership from this day forward? Will you use it for yourself? Build a nice career, vacation when you want, establish a strong nest egg, retire early, and die peacefully?

Or will you use your leadership for impact, invest in your family and others, sacrifice time for causes you believe in, give your money generously, die with a legacy that left nothing on the table, and change the world in the process?

My hope is that you'll choose the latter and become a leader of impact.

ABOUT LEADERIMPACT

I wrote this book in partnership with LeaderImpact. I've been volunteering, speaking, leading groups, and have been involved on a global level for a number of years.

When I say you need to find a cause and dive in, for me, this is it. I love seeing leaders engaged in becoming leaders of impact. There's no better gift they could give to the world.

LeaderImpact has been inspiring and developing leaders for decades. Their purpose as a global organization is to help leaders develop professionally, personally, and spiritually in order to have an impact.

Leaders meet together in groups on a regular basis to work through LeaderImpact curriculum, which is typically based on popular business and leadership books by authors such as Jim Collins, Patrick Lencioni, Simon Sinek, and others. Groups are facilitated by volunteer leaders who have great real-world experience and who buy in to the core values of the organization.

What sets LeaderImpact apart from the myriad of networking

or peer groups is their focus on holistic development for the leader (professional, personal, and spiritual) and their focus on outreach. It's not enough for leaders to stay insulated in these groups. It's about growth and inviting other leaders to experience the same life change.

Each city runs LeaderImpact forums, which are events designed to bring together the influential leaders within an area. These forums typically feature a great speaker in an upscale or cool venue to ensure a great experience.

Each year, there are multiple trips to countries that are starting LeaderImpact. Experienced leaders have the opportunity to present great content from their area of expertise but also share where impact comes from. I've had the privilege of speaking and working with leaders in numerous countries around the world. I'd love for you to experience the same thing.

Even though the organization is active in over twenty-five countries, it's still in its infancy stage. We need great leaders, like you, to get on board and leverage your time, influence, and resources to propel it forward.

This is what being part of a movement is about. You can help us.

Sometimes you just need a little push.

You can find out more, start a group, or get involved at LeaderImpact.com.

ACKNOWLEDGMENTS

This is the first book I've written. It took more time than I thought and more help from others than I imagined.

Firstly, I want to thank my most important relationship, my amazing wife, Jen. I love you. This book robbed us of time together often, and I thank you for your understanding, encouragement, and editing. I couldn't have done this without your support, and I'm so thankful that you're my wife. I know that I owe you a great vacation...or three.

Rylan and London. You fill my life with joy and energy. Thank you for inspiring me to be a great dad and being patient as I wrote this. Your interruptions into my office as I write are always welcome. I love you to pieces.

To the team at LeaderImpact that worked hard to bring this book to life—thank you! Roger Osbaldiston and Judy Hildebrandt for your input, wisdom, and connections. You both also reviewed drafts in record time. Nathan Hildebrandt for pushing this project forward, raising support, and making it happen. Preston Wieler for your continued support and input over the years and Katie Bircham Carpintero for keeping us on task and helping with the assessment. You all rock.

My Douglas fam. Dad and Mom, thank you for the years of endless support, encouragement, and prayer. You're amazing parents and a great standard to live up to. To my sister Marnie and brother Nate—thanks for letting the world peek into our lives growing up and for the great stories and wisdom that you've supplied me with over the years. You're amazing people and siblings. I know I just scratched the surface too. Love you guys.

Thank you, Josh and Christine Cairns, for being all in with us. Your friendship and partnership runs deep in all areas of life.

The CREW. Thanks, Sujina Unger, for your help in the assessment and all the LeaderImpact stuff I get your help with. Thanks, Rose Atkinson, for being my assistant for years. Trying to keep me organized on top of writing must have driven you crazy at times. Thanks, Justin Sherwin, for your design chops and, Dan Ryu, for your creative direction. And to the rest of the CREW that let me take time to write this, thanks for being golden plungers. Also, thanks to the first plunger at CREW, Hakon Fauske, for your friendship and passion.

Thank you to the great people at Scribe Media. Tucker, Zach, Hal the chief, Cristina, Emily, Tashan, Rachael, and the rest of the team. You took a marketer and created an author. That is your genius.

To the leaders and their stories in the book. Thanks for giving me your time, authenticity, and for being leaders of impact every day.

Thanks Stu McLaren and Jeremy Laidlaw for being great roommates in university and lifelong friends. You were instrumental in ensuring I walked the path of leadership early. I'm always inspired by who you are and what you're doing in the world.

Sorry, Huijo, for calling you "Tricky" for years.

To the leaders in my LeaderImpact group, thanks for your friendship and encouragement. There's more to come.

This process was long but worth it. I may even write another book, but I won't try pole vaulting ever again.

LEADERIMPACT ASSESSMENT

Read and reflect on the questions as you answer them. Circle the corresponding number from 1 to 5 beside your answer. Subtotal the section, and then add up all three sections for your total score.

Remember that there is no right or wrong answer. It's just an assessment to understand where you are today. The goal is to see progress in the areas that are important to you and that help you become a leader who makes an impact. If you fill this assessment out again in a year or two from now, my hope is that you'll see improvement and that it will encourage you to keep going.

PROFESSIONAL LIFE

1) HOW DO YOU FEEL ABOUT YOUR WORK?

1. I dislike my work and am actively looking for other opportunities.
2. I like my work but don't see a long-term fit.
3. I enjoy my work and feel comfortable.
4. I love my work and feel fulfilled by my job activities.

5. My work is the perfect outflow of who I am, and it allows me to live out my values and passion.

2) ARE YOU ACTIVELY INVESTING IN YOUR PROFESSIONAL DEVELOPMENT?

1. No—I allow my daily circumstances and tasks to dictate what I focus my attention on.
2. Yes—professional skills only.
3. Yes—professional and soft skills.
4. I take advantage of most development opportunities available.
5. I actively invest my own time and resources in my professional development.

3) WHAT IS YOUR GREATEST MOTIVATOR AT WORK?

1. I am not motivated at all.
2. My current work is simply a job; I am there for the money.
3. I generally enjoy my work, and it provides for my family.
4. I believe my work is a great match with my skills, abilities, and passion. It is enjoyable.
5. My work is an outflow of who I am; I am completely fulfilled in my work.

4) HOW WOULD YOU DESCRIBE YOUR WORK-LIFE BALANCE?

1. Terrible—I am always working, and it is bad for me and my family.
2. Not great—My work occupies my thoughts much of the time when I am off.
3. OK—I'm invested in my work but am able to compartmentalize it when necessary.
4. Good—I leave my work at the office.

5. Excellent—My work is a natural outflow of who I am, and therefore, the balance of life is natural.

5) DO YOU HAVE THE REQUIRED SKILLS TO EXCEL AT WORK?

1. No—I struggle daily with the work I am involved in.
2. I'm competent enough to not lose my job.
3. I'm learning and finding myself more confident each day.
4. I am skilled at what I do and feel good about my contribution.
5. I am at the top of my field.

6) DO YOU HAVE A MENTOR AT WORK?

1. No—I work primarily on my own, without professional guidance.
2. I have a supervisor, but he/she only engages with me when I ask questions.
3. I have a supervisor who takes an active role in my vocational growth.
4. I have a mentor who is concerned both with my development as an employee and individual.
5. I have a mentor who is fully committed to my development in all aspects of my life and work.

7) ARE YOU MENTORING ANYONE AT WORK?

1. No—Not formally.
2. Yes—As part of my supervisory responsibilities.
3. Yes—I see it as my role to develop my staff not only professionally but also personally.
4. Yes—I actively seek out opportunities to invest in the lives of the next generation.

5. Yes—I believe that my primary role in my workplace is to mentor others personally, professionally, and spiritually.

8) HOW DO YOU SEE YOUR LEVEL OF COMPENSATION AT WORK?

1. I am significantly underpaid.
2. I am underpaid, but this is due to my relative inexperience.
3. I earn an average salary for my level of experience.
4. I am compensated fairly and have opportunities to progress.
5. I am compensated very well for the work I perform and have opportunities to progress.

9) HOW SATISFIED ARE YOU WITH YOUR LEVEL OF COMPENSATION?

1. I feel significantly undervalued, and it affects my motivation and self-worth.
2. I wish I were compensated higher but understand this is a season for growth and development.
3. I feel that my compensation is appropriate for the value I provide.
4. I am satisfied with what I earn.
5. I am compensated very well and consider it a blessing to be valued by my employer.

10) DO YOU HAVE PROFESSIONAL GOALS AT WORK?

1. No—I do not currently have anything that I would like to work toward.
2. I have some loose ideas of things I would like to accomplish.
3. I set goals each year but rarely follow through.
4. I set goals that I am mostly committed to and try to accomplish them.

5. I set significant professional goals that act as guideposts for decision-making.

Subtotal: _____

PERSONAL LIFE

11) HOW WOULD YOU DESCRIBE YOUR SLEEP HABITS?

1. Terrible—I never sleep well.
2. Not great—I don't get enough sleep at night and am lethargic throughout the day.
3. Adequate—I get six to seven hours of sleep.
4. Good—I generally sleep well and feel recharged and energized for the next day.
5. Excellent—I fall asleep quickly and sleep soundly. I maintain a regular sleep routine, which keeps me well rested.

12) DO YOU SPEND TIME ACTIVELY INVESTING IN PERSONAL DEVELOPMENT (READING, MARRIAGE RETREATS, FITNESS GROUPS, OR TRAINING, ETC.)?

1. No—Personal development is not a priority for me.
2. I invest minimal time in personal development.
3. I spend enough time/energy to feel like I am not falling behind in life.
4. Personal growth and development are important to me, and I make them yearly priorities.
5. I have significant goals for my personal growth and invest heavily in my development.

13) HOW WOULD DESCRIBE YOUR GENERAL MOOD (SELF-THOUGHTS AND SELF-TALK)?

1. I have a very negative outlook on life and often feel hopeless.
2. I am often sad and lacking energy.
3. I have good days and bad.
4. I am generally happy and upbeat.
5. I am almost always happy and optimistic.

14) HOW WELL ARE YOU ABLE TO HANDLE ANXIETY, STRESS, AND FEAR? ARE YOU ABLE TO CONCENTRATE AND WORK WELL UNDER PRESSURE?

1. I constantly feel overwhelmed by emotional stressors.
2. I generally handle daily pressures well but am thrown off by any significant change or stress.
3. I am productive during periods of stress, but it affects my well-being.
4. I have a good ability to handle the stresses of life and work and am effective in the midst of trials and pressures.
5. I have proactive strategies in place to manage what life throws at me and am able to focus in any situation.

15) HOW CAPABLE ARE YOU OF SEEING FROM THE PERSPECTIVE OF ANOTHER PERSON DURING A DISAGREEMENT?

1. I don't understand other people. I only see things my way.
2. I am occasionally aware of the perspectives of others, but don't understand how they arrive at their conclusions.
3. I understand and balance multiple perspectives in my decision-making and response to disagreement.
4. I actively seek out other perspectives and try to make decisions that are appropriate to all involved.
5. I constantly view situations from an objective and empathetic point of view.

16) HOW WOULD YOU DESCRIBE YOUR EMOTIONAL MANAGEMENT (OUTWARD EXPRESSION OF INWARD FEELINGS)?

1. I struggle to control my outbursts.
2. I have limited control over my emotions and am easily provoked.
3. During periods of stress, my ability to manage my emotions is compromised.
4. I am on a pretty even keel most of the time.
5. Self-control is a core character trait of mine.

17) HOW WOULD YOUR FAMILY MEMBERS RATE YOUR DEDICATION OF TIME AND ATTENTION TO YOUR FAMILY?

1. I don't have a family. (N/A)
2. I am emotionally and physically distant.
3. I am not as available as my family would like, but they understand this is a season of life.
4. I try to be present and attentive whenever possible.
5. My family is very important to me. I dedicate significant time and attention to them.

18) HOW WOULD YOUR SPOUSE/PARTNER RATE YOUR DEDICATION OF TIME AND ATTENTION TO YOUR MARRIAGE/PARTNERSHIP?

1. I am not married or in a committed relationship at this time. (N/A)
2. I am emotionally and physically distant.
3. I am not as available as my spouse/partner would like, but they understand this is a season of life.
4. I try to be present and attentive whenever possible.
5. My spouse/partner is very important to me. I dedicate significant time and attention to him/her.

19) HOW WOULD YOU DESCRIBE YOUR FRIENDSHIPS?

1. Maintaining friendships is not a priority for me. (N/A)
2. I don't really have any friends.
3. I have many acquaintances but no true friendships.
4. I have one or two very close friends.
5. I have a number of long-term, deep friendships.

20) HOW DO YOU FEEL ABOUT YOUR GENERAL PHYSICAL HEALTH AND FITNESS?

1. My current physical well-being puts me at medical risk.
2. I am physically unhealthy and am not happy about it.
3. I could be in better condition, but I exert minimal effort.
4. I am in decent shape and exercise whenever I have the time.
5. I value my physical health and actively pursue it.

21) HOW ARE YOUR NUTRITIONAL HABITS?

1. I have very poor nutritional habits, and improving is not a priority for me.
2. I have poor nutritional habits but am aware of them and would like to improve.
3. I have average nutritional habits. I try to make healthy choices.
4. I have good nutritional habits. I make a conscious effort to eat well and am quite disciplined.
5. Excellent—I am informed nutritionally and follow a nutritional plan that is optimal for my lifestyle.

22) DO YOU HAVE GOALS FOR YOUR PERSONAL LIFE?

1. No, I do not currently have any personal goals.

2. I have no specific goals set but have loose ideas of what I would like to accomplish.
3. I set goals each year but rarely follow through.
4. I set goals that I am committed to and try my best to accomplish them.
5. I regularly set personal goals and almost always achieve them.

Subtotal: _____

SPIRITUAL LIFE

23) DO YOU HAVE A SATISFYING SENSE OF PURPOSE IN YOUR LIFE?

1. I've lost a true sense of purpose in my life.
2. I'm struggling to find meaning and purpose but remain hopeful.
3. Only occasionally do I sense purpose.
4. I often feel that I have purpose in certain areas of my life.
5. I have a deep sense of purpose in all aspects of my life.

24) HOW WOULD YOU DESCRIBE YOUR SPIRITUAL LIFE/HEALTH AT THIS POINT?

1. I do not know/believe in God.
2. I feel disconnected from God.
3. I wish I felt more connected to God.
4. I feel connected to God.
5. I am constantly aware of the presence of God in my life.

25) HOW FREQUENTLY ARE YOU CURRENTLY EXPERIENCING JOY IN YOUR LIFE?

1. Not at all.

2. I'm in a season of trial and weariness but am hopeful that it will pass.
3. Hit and miss. Some days are great, and others are not.
4. I experience joy most of the time, but I'd like to experience it more often.
5. I'm consistently joyful with others, affirming the trait within me.

26) HOW WOULD YOU EVALUATE YOUR CAPACITY FOR PATIENCE?

1. Very poor—I'm consistently angry with delays or mistakes.
2. I'm restless and get irritated easily.
3. It's a work in progress.
4. I'm typically well restrained but have the occasional lapse.
5. Patience is a core character trait of mine.

27) HOW OFTEN DO YOU FEEL COMPASSION OR ACT COMPASSIONATELY TOWARD OTHERS?

1. Very rarely—My focus tends to remain solely on myself.
2. I only occasionally show kindness and compassion to others.
3. I often try to be compassionate, but it doesn't come naturally.
4. I'm often kind and compassionate toward others.
5. I regularly seek ways to show kindness or compassion to others.

28) HOW OFTEN DO YOU FEEL LOVED OR SHOW LOVE TOWARD OTHERS?

1. I rarely show love to others, and they rarely show love toward me.
2. Infrequently—But I desire it more.

3. Occasionally—But there's room for improvement.
4. I often love others and feel loved in return.
5. Love is a regular aspect of my life, and this is reciprocated by others.

29) HOW IS YOUR PRAYER LIFE?

1. I don't pray.
2. I say a prayer before meals.
3. I pray daily for people and things that are important to me.
4. I am in active communication with God throughout the day.
5. I am a prayer warrior and spend more than five hours a week in prayer.

30) HOW IS YOUR LEVEL OF SELF-CONTROL?

1. Very poor—I'm not in control of my thoughts/actions.
2. Not great—Circumstances or situations often dictate my responses.
3. Variable—It's a work in progress.
4. I typically exercise strong self-control with rare lapses.
5. Self-control is a core character trait of mine.

31) ARE YOUR THOUGHTS AND ACTIONS CONSISTENT WITH A HIGH MORAL STANDARD?

1. No—I have a lot of room for improvement.
2. They could be better.
3. Sometimes—But I am focusing on improving.
4. I consistently act morally but struggle with my thoughts.
5. My thoughts and actions are both consistently moral, with very rare lapses.

32) HOW IMPORTANT IS SPIRITUAL GROWTH AND DEVELOPMENT TO YOU?

1. Not important at all.
2. Somewhat important.
3. Important—But I'm not actively pursuing it.
4. I am looking for more of this.
5. I am actively engaged in spiritual growth.

Subtotal: _____

Professional Life Total: _____

Personal Life Total: _____

Spiritual Life Total: _____

Grand Total: _____

HOW DO YOU COMPARE?

I love working with leaders because they're driven and competitive. They're also insecure, and they compare themselves against other leaders or businesses or organizations. This assessment is not a clinical diagnosis of your professional, personal, and spiritual health. There's no winner or loser, or better or worse. Rather, it's an opportunity for you to evaluate how you currently feel about various aspects of your life. It's a measure of progress over time. My hope is that you constantly move forward and are intentional about developing areas that you feel need to be improved.

From our survey with over five hundred leaders from various parts of the world, here are the average scores.

	PERSONAL (OUT OF 60)	PROFESSIONAL (OUT OF 50)	SPIRITUAL (OUT OF 50)	TOTAL SCORE (OUT OF 160)
ALL LEADERS	45	35	40	120
CEO/PRESIDENT	47	39	41	127
OWNER/ ENTREPRENEUR	45	36	39	120
SR. MANAGEMENT (VP, DIRECTOR)	45	35	39	120
MANAGEMENT (SUPERVISOR, TEAM LEAD)	45	34	40	118
EMPLOYEE	44	33	40	117
OTHER	43	32	39	114
RETIRED	46	35	41	122
MALE	45	35	39	120
FEMALE	44	35	41	120

Note: Sample Size = 537 completed responses (September 2019)

It's always interesting to see where our scores stand.

If you like where you are, great. It's important to maintain that level in each area and stay sharp. You are also able to help others who are not there yet. That might mean teaching, mentoring, and building into other leaders in a very intentional way.

If you're not happy with your scores, you get to work on them. The goal in life is not perfection but progress.

The introductory component to LeaderImpact is called Foundations. It's typically four to five sessions in which you work through your life history, values, purpose, vision, and goal setting. The assessment is also part of the Foundations program and helps you take the next steps.

The best part is reviewing your assessment with other leaders in a group environment. I've personally been through it multiple times in groups, and I've always learned new perspectives and insights that you can apply to your life. It will make you a sharper leader and better person.

ABOUT THE AUTHOR

BRADEN DOUGLAS is the founder of CREW Marketing Partners, one of the fastest-growing marketing and creative agencies in Canada, with multiple locations. Founded in 2007, CREW has won numerous awards and worked with some of the best brands.

As one of the youngest marketers hired at Procter & Gamble and then Frito-Lay, Braden did something that many of his colleagues considered a career-limiting move. He left the corporate world. He followed his passion to work with a national nonprofit organization called Campus Crusade for Christ, which is now known as Power to Change. It was at this nonprofit that he developed his proprietary marketing strategy framework and model of agency. More importantly, he realized the potential and ability for leaders to make a significant impact in the world.

It was this desire that led to starting CREW.

His passion and purpose are to help leaders find true success. CREW focuses on business results, and his volunteer work through LeaderImpact focuses on helping leaders live a life of impact. He speaks at events to audiences across North America and around the world and writes regularly through social media and online at BradenDouglas.com.

He lives outside Vancouver, British Columbia, with his wife and two kids. He's an avid reader, volunteer, writer, and athlete who runs, plays soccer, snowboards, and is constantly active with his family.

NOTES

1   John C. Maxwell, *The 21 Irrefutable Laws of Leadership* (Nashville: Thomas Nelson, 1998).

2   "Civil Rights Icon Rosa Parks Dies at 92," CNN, October 25, 2005, https://www.cnn.com/2005/US/10/25/parks.obit/index.html.

3   Taken from Matthew 13:3–8. Eugene Peterson, *The Message Paraphrased Bible* (Colorado Springs, CO: NavPress, 2018)

4   Greg McKeown, *Essentialism: The Disciplined Pursuit of Less* (New York: Crown, 2014), 131.

5   Chris Weller and Skye Gould, "Here Are the Ages You Peak at Everything in your Life," *Business Insider*, October 5, 2017.

6   Eric J. Olson, "Healthy Lifestyle: Adult Health: Expert Answers: How Many Hours of Sleep Are Enough for Good Health?" Mayo Clinic, June 6, 2019, https://www.mayoclinic.org/healthy-lifestyle/adult-health/expert-answers/how-many-hours-of-sleep-are-enough/faq-20057898.

7   "Healthy Sleep: Benefits of Sleep," Division of Sleep Medicine at Harvard Medical School, http://healthysleep.med.harvard.edu/healthy/matters/benefits-of-sleep.

8   Earlexia Norwood, "The Surprising Health Benefits of Smiling," *Henry Ford Live Well* (blog), October 5, 2017.

9   Tim Keller, *The Prodigal God* (New York: Dutton Press, 2008), 60.

10 Matthew 16:24–26 (New Living Translation).

11 John 15:12–13 (New American Standard).

12 Matthew 22:37 (New Living Translation).

13   Matthew 22:38 (New Living Translation).

14   Galatians 5:22–23 (New Living Translation).

15   1 Corinthians 13:4–7 (New Living Translation).

16   John 15:5 (New Living Translation).

17   James Allen, *As a Man Thinketh* (1908).

18   "Three-Quarters of Millennials Would Take a Pay Cut to Work for a Socially
     Responsible Company, according to Research from Cone Communications," Cone
     Communications, November 2, 2016, https://www.prnewswire.com/news-releases/
     three-quarters-of-millennials-would-take-a-pay-cut-to-work-for-a-socially-responsible-company-
     according-to-research-from-cone-communications-300355311.html.

19   V. Kasturi, Lisa Chase, and Sohel Karim, "The Truth about CSR," *Harvard Business Review*
     (January–February 2015), https://hbr.org/2015/01/the-truth-about-csr.

20   "Will Consumers Pay More for Products from Socially Responsible Companies?" *Marketing
     Charts*, October 15, 2015, https://www.marketingcharts.com/brand-related-60166.

21   "Nearly All Consumers Likely to Switch Brands to Support a Cause This Holiday Season," Cone
     Communications, December 1, 2011, https://www.prnewswire.com/news-releases/nearly-all-
     consumers-likely-to-switch-brands-to-support-a-cause-this-holiday-season-134834278.html.

22   Jim Collins, *Good to Great: Why Some Companies Make the Leap and Others Don't* (New York:
     HarperCollins, 2001).

23   Proverbs 15:22 (New Living Translation).

24   Taken from Exodus 3:9–12, Eugene Peterson, *The Message Paraphrased Bible* (Colorado Springs,
     CO: NavPress).

Printed in Great Britain
by Amazon

17317679R00135